Rambling with Gill

James Gill

ZAGAT PUBLISHING • NEW YORK

DEDICATION

This book is dedicated
to the memory of my late dear friend,
B.J. Harrington,
who was the finest Catholic layman
I've ever known.*

The proceeds of this book
will go to his favorite charity,

The Elizabeth Seton Pediatric Center,
in the name of my granddaughter,
Gillian Rose Hearn.

* Attached as Appendix A is a copy of a speech I delivered at Fordham Law School when B.J. was honored on September 26, 2010, at an Evening of Remembrance.

INTRODUCTION

I've lived a long life and enjoyed a host of varied experiences and interesting people.

As a result, I've developed a myriad of thoughts on subjects and people which I want to share with others before I die.

This is my third book. I've written two previous ones: "For James and Gillian," my grandchildren and "Speaking of Gill," which is a discussion of public speaking.

I enjoyed writing both of them and this one as well. This time, I've written a sort of stream of consciousness to be picked up and laid down without reference to what you've read or not read before.

You may well disagree with some of my views and I respect that – but you will have no trouble discerning what my views are!

FOREWARD by Ed Koch

Jim Gill and I met in the early 70s through our mutual friend, Allen Schwartz, now deceased. Allen and Jim had both been Assistant District Attorneys in the Manhattan DA's office under the leadership of Mr. Frank Hogan. Hogan, now a legendary figure, was never addressed or referred to without the salutation "Mr." (Jim recently told me that his starting salary in that position was $4,000.)

When Allen left the DA's office in 1962 to become my law partner in the firm of Koch & Schwartz, he, Jim and I continued our friendship. Allen later served as Corporation Counsel during my first term as mayor, and Jim provided sound advice to me during that time as well. Jim also served for a time as a special investigator of misconduct and impropriety in the New York City school system, including improper involvement with schoolchildren.

I knew I had a special friend and had chosen the right guy to conduct the investigation when I saw Jim on television telling a reporter, "If that guy [a witness before him] had done to my daughter what he did to that student, I would have shot him between the eyes with a gun."

When I was leaving my position as Mayor of New York City, having served for 12 years from 1978 through 1989, I was looking to return to the practice of law. I had given up that practice in 1968 when I was elected to Congress where I stayed through 1977 when I was elected mayor. Jim brought me into the law firm where he was a partner, now known as Bryan Cave LLP. For the past 21 years, we have had lunch together about three times a week. We never bore one another, which is amazing to me, since we have undoubtedly retold our best stories many times over the years.

Jim and I are alike in many ways. We were both raised in poverty and we both have a great sense of humor. Yet in many ways we are very different, and our philosophies on life often differ. I am a secular

Jew who believes in God and reward and punishment in the hereafter. I expect to be rewarded. Jim is a very strict Catholic. His Catholicism draws the red lines in his life. He makes it clear, always with a smile, that his life is dominated by a love of God and a willingness to revere "He who must be obeyed." (A reference to His Holiness the Pope, as well as to Cardinals and Archbishops.) Jim is a lawyer for the Archdiocese of New York. As a result of that position, and my having been mayor, we both became good friends with John Cardinal O'Connor, Edward Cardinal Egan, and the current Archbishop of New York, Timothy Dolan.

Jim has a lovely family. It includes his wife, Jackie, an independent-minded woman and a terrific cook. His daughter, Rose, serves as Commissioner of the Department of Investigation in Mayor Bloomberg's Administration and is married to Frank Hearn. Rose and Frank have two children: James and Gillian. Jim also has two sons: Dennis and Patrick. Patrick and his wife, Nancie, have a daughter, Julia.

Another great passion in Jim's life is the United States Marines in which he served as a legal officer in the late 1950s. He has told me endlessly that, in addition to his family and his Catholic faith, being a Marine is his proudest achievement.

I believe Jim's major red line in living his life comes out of the Irish potato famine of 1845 and the fact that Irishmen suffering hunger from the famine went to English soup kitchens. They were lectured and hectored about Irish failures and viewed as weaklings by their neighbors who referred to them as having "taken the soup." Jim will never compromise on matters of conscience, and for that alone, I love him.

"Rambling With Gill," Jim's third book, is dedicated to his friend, B.J. Harrington. But I believe Jim's purpose in writing the book was to lay out for his grandson, James, the red lines that would guide James's life as he enters adulthood. Citing his earliest memories and experiences and his reactions to them in this book is his way of providing James with the wisdom of the ages, as imparted by Lord Chesterton to his son and Shakespeare's Polonius to Laertes.

I am sure that James will listen well and later on in life realize how fortunate he was to have this extraordinary granddad who loved him and shared so much of his time and wisdom with him. Jim has imparted eternal values and provided James with an understanding of respect, love and insight into the greatness of his Irish heritage and Roman Catholic faith.

Jim and I have pledged to one another that whomever survives the other, he will speak at the other's funeral. The likelihood is that I will hear him speak at mine, since I am 86 and he is 79. In addition to all else, Jim is a great speaker and I am looking forward to the roast.

My father was a lifelong member of the Machinist Workers Union and a shop steward at Scoville Manufacturing Company in Waterbury, Connecticut, my hometown. He went to work after the 6th Grade. He was the eldest child in his family and had to take care of the needs of his siblings. He worked at Scoville all of his life except for two stints in the U.S. Navy. He served as a Machinist Mate in the engine room of a destroyer, operating in the Atlantic Ocean during World War I.

This is my father's "engine room" crew during World War I. He is the last one in the front row on the right.

During World War II, he served as a Chief Petty Officer at the Great Lakes Training Station teaching young sailors how to be machinists mates aboard U.S. ships.

He did not have to go into the service during World War II because he was over age, but chose to do so. On Sunday, December 7, 1941, we went to the movies. When we came out, news of the attack on Pearl Harbor was posted on all the telephone poles. I never saw my father so angry. He said to me: "Our country has been attacked by the 'Japs' and it's my job to defend it." He was back in the Navy within months. His great disappointment was that he was sent to the Great Lakes Training Station to teach instead of being assigned to a ship of the line. If he had been assigned to a ship, he would have had command of its engine room, and that's what he wanted!

During the war there were severe shortages of many things, particularly gas and meat. When my father came home on leave, from the Great Lakes, he would bring with him suitcases full of meats of all kinds. If we had owned a car, he probably would have found some way to bring home gas as well! He knew how to get around. He was part of Tom Brokaw's "Great Generation."

This is my father's unit at the Great Lakes during World War II. He is sitting in the front row, second from the left.

The culture of our country has changed since then. I wonder whether we could ever mount the magnificent effort we mounted during World War II. Let's hope that it never becomes necessary.

I learned two things from my father: Love of country and the importance of the union movement.

There is a great deal I don't know about my father because my mother died when I was four years old and I was raised by my mother's sister, my Aunt Nell. My mother had asked my Aunt Nell to do so when she was dying because she knew that my father would have to continue working at Scoville and would not be able to take care of me.

My Aunt Nell was married to John Golden when she took me in and her father, my maternal grandfather, lived with her as well. Later she had a son, my cousin, Jack Golden, who is really a brother to me since we grew up together under the same roof and love each other as brothers. We lived on the second floor of a three family house at 44 Plaza Avenue.

The most frightening thing that happened to me during my boyhood was when my friend, Farrell Connor, and I inadvertently set fire to the Lincoln Street Woods.

We had been playing with matches in the woods during the fall and the fire we started suddenly got out of hand. As the fire grew larger and larger and started moving toward a large group of automobile garages, I started running with all my strength to the Fire House at the top of Willow Street, ½ mile away and all uphill. On arrival, I burst into the Fire House and shouted "The Lincoln Street Woods are on fire." They asked me my name and where I lived. I told them and ran all the way home; told my Aunt Nell what had happened and literally hid under my bed, convinced that the firemen would come after me to send me to jail. My Aunt's assurances that everything would be "all right" were of no avail.

The firemen put the fire out before it reached the garages and never came after me. Although I am certain they knew I had started the fire,

I think they gave me a pass because I reported it as described. You could do that in those days – it was a different era.

The most embarrassing experience of my boyhood took place when I went on a long hike in the woods with some friends. After a while I had to go to the bathroom and of course, there was none. Accordingly, I went in the woods and made the dreadful mistake of wiping myself with Poison Ivy!

The result was horrendous and my Aunt Nell encased my entire rear end in Calamine lotion, which I had to wear for weeks.

I'm sure that my incessant scratching during that period caused considerable puzzlement and speculation among those unaware of my condition. In any event to this day whenever I see Poison Ivy, I grab my rear end and go the other way!

Probably the most exciting thing that occurred during my boyhood was when I opened a lemonade stand on a very hot day at the beginning of summer. My Aunt Nell made the lemonade, which was delicious, and my grandfather, "Gramp" as I used to call him, observed my entrepreneurial skills from across the street.

Sometime during the course of the day, a photographer from the Waterbury Republican American newspaper arrived on the scene and took my picture, which appeared in the paper the next day! I was overjoyed as were my Aunt Nell and "Gramp." It was at that moment that I developed my lifelong, insatiable desire for public adulation!

"Gramp" was a very wise man and taught me a host of basic principles. He taught me to be polite and to respect other people – all other people. He taught me never to forget to say "Thank you." It angers me to this day when others fail to do so, particularly when the "thanks" are due and owing to me! He told me never to be awed by people with money or power, and I never have been. He urged me to work 10 percent harder than my closest competitor and imparted numerous other lessens as well.

I in turn have passed those lessons on to my grandson, James, both verbally and in writing and he has responded to them just as I did to my grandfather's teachings. "Gramp" and I were very close as are James and I. In addition, whenever I read a worthwhile book, I summarize it in the form of a letter to James.

"Gramp" was tall and erect. He smoked a pipe and wore high shoes, laced to the top. He had a long kindly face and spoke softly. He always had a roll of peppermint "Life Savers" on his person which he shared with me.

This is "Gramp".

In retrospect it is clear that my Aunt Nell viewed her guardianship of me as a sacred trust due and owing to my mother whom she adored. She protected and promoted me without limitation.

Mother's Day was however, a somewhat uneasy day for me. On that day, all children wore a red rose in deference to their mothers. Because my mother had died I wore a white rose in accordance with the practice of the time. I was the only one in my class who wore a white rose and it made me feel kind of peculiar. But, of course, I wore it in deference to my mother and Aunt Nell would have it no other way.

When my mother died, my father moved in with his sister, my Aunt Marcy, who was married and had three children. She was a short, stout, tough lady. Her husband, Bill Neville, was a big strapping "over the road" truck driver who would catch her wrath and indeed her punches whenever he had too much to drink! But she had a heart of gold and she loved my father and me as we did her.

My father had two other sisters, my Aunts Anne and Helen, both of whom became nurses and two brothers, Tom and Ed, both of whom established their own businesses and did well. The success of my father's siblings was at least in part due to his going to work at an early age to help his father, my grandfather, support the family. My paternal grandfather was the janitor at St. Anne's Church in Waterbury. That's all I know about him and I know nothing about my paternal grandmother.

And so as a young boy I would be with my father on weekends until he re-enlisted in the Navy during World War II. By the time he was discharged I was away at a prep school in Lenox, Massachusetts. After prep school I went away to Holy Cross College in Worcester, Massachusetts, and moved to New York City with my Aunt Nell. And so I grew up among my mother's people, the Shanahans – my grandfather, my uncles, aunts and cousins.

I remember very little about my mother except that when she was dying of pneumonia at St. Mary's Hospital in Waterbury she asked to see me. I went to St. Mary's Hospital for what was a final visit and sensed very strongly that there was something terribly wrong although I didn't know what it was.

When I grew older I learned about my mother. She was the eldest in her family, very bright and had an exceptional sense of humor. She was elegant and not prone to cooking or house work, which she left to my Aunt Nell. She took over the running of the Shanahan family when her mother died. She was fiercely loyal to family members and took extraordinary care of her two youngest brothers, Tom and Dennis. My daughter Rose is named for her and has many of her qualities.

This is my mother.

I could not have had a better mother than my Aunt Nell or a happier boyhood. St. Margaret's Parish was the center of all activity. In those days the mass was said in Latin. I learned all of the Latin responses and served as an altar boy. I played on St. Margaret's basketball team and was the captain of our baseball team. On Sundays I attended mass with my classmates. Holy days were major events celebrated in extraordinary ways. There were three sit down family meals every day – breakfast, lunch and dinner.

I would go to New York on the train with "Gramp" almost every Sunday to visit with my uncles, aunts and cousins usually at my Uncle Ed's apartment in Astoria, Queens, where lengthy and sometimes heated political discussions took place. My bachelor uncles John and Dennis came to Waterbury every year to spend the Christmas holidays with us. My Uncle John was a book-maker who plied his trade in Philadelphia, and my Uncle Dennis founded the Shanahan Construction Company in Ellenville, New York. My Uncle Dennis was exceptionally bright and went to Notre Dame. He was the first in our family to attend college. He was quiet, private and a deeply religious Catholic. He had a huge influence on me.

Ringling Brothers Circus would come to Waterbury once a year and I would work together with other kids preparing the circus grounds for which we received free tickets for a performance. (The first year I reported to work for the circus I was turned down because I was "too small" and I was furious.)

During the summer it was baseball every day, morning, afternoon and night.

There was no television and the main sources of entertainment were the movies, the radio, the funny papers and comic books.

The movie stars of the day included Humphrey Bogart, Clark Gable, Jimmy Stewart, Bette Davis, Joan Crawford, Sidney Greenstreet, Peter Lorre, Jimmy Cagney, Fred Astaire, Rita Hayworth, Betty Grable, Edgar G. Robinson, Henry Fonda, Gary Cooper, Ava Gardner, Katherine Hepburn, Judy Garland, Mickey Rooney, Lana Turner and Susan Haywood. My favorites were Bogart, Stewart, Greenstreet, Lorre, Cagney and as I got a little older, Rita Hayworth and Lana Turner.

My favorite radio show was "I Love a Mystery," my favorite comic strip character was "Dick Tracy," and my favorite comic book was "Batman."

I earned pocket money by peddling newspapers from house to house in the early morning hours. I would receive my bundle of papers at the corner of Plaza Avenue and Willow Street and would fold them into "scalers," which enabled me to scale the papers onto the porches of customers from the street. I became very adept at that form of delivery and never broke a window! The paper I peddled was the "Waterbury Republican American." Bill Pape was a classmate at St. Margaret's and his father owned the "Waterbury Republican American." Bill Pape now publishes the paper and we are friends.

All in all, it was a great life.

I began the First Grade at St. Margaret's Grammar School in Water-bury, in September 1937.

My teacher was Sister Mary Frederick of the Sisters of Mercy. All of my teachers at St. Margaret's were nuns except for Miss Delany who taught Second Grade and Miss Phalen who taught Fourth Grade. They were all magnificent and I received an extraordinary basic education.

You will be surprised to learn and I am delighted to tell you that Sister Mary Frederick is alive and well!

I communicate with her regularly and brought her and one of her companions down from Connecticut for lunch at the "21" Club. She is a "rip" and we had a fantastic time. I still remember her standing in front of our First Grade class and she still remembers me sitting in the front row and asking all sorts of questions.

God bless Sister Mary Frederick and all nuns throughout the world. Think of all of their unstinting and selfless good works down through the years in the fields of education, medical care and caring for the poor – all for the love of God and nothing more!

Time and again I've heard stories about the nuns cracking students on the knuckles with rulers. All I can tell you is that it never happened to me or anyone else to my knowledge during my 8 years at St. Margaret's. By and large I think those are stories made out of whole cloth by persons interested in convincing others of how "tough" they had it. Nor did I ever hear of a priest engaging in sexual abuse of a child.

On Sunday, July 18, 2010, I returned to Waterbury to participate in the celebration of the 100th anniversary of St. Margaret's Parish. My friend, Archbishop Henry Mansell, the Archbishop of Hartford, said the celebration mass at the newly renovated St. Margaret's Church.

I arranged for Sister Mary Frederick to attend with some of her companions and it was a spectacular event! I don't know how old Sister

Mary Frederick is and I dare not ask but she is just as spry and alert as she was when she taught me in the first grade more than 70 years ago!

This is Sister Mary Frederick.

I first met Archbishop Henry Mansell when he served in the Archdiocese of New York under Cardinal O'Connor. As a matter of fact, I attended the first mass he celebrated at St. Patrick's Cathedral as a bishop. During the course of that mass the newly consecrated Bishop utilized Cardinal O'Connor's Episcopal chair and Cardinal O'Connor occupied a lesser station on the other side of the altar. When the Cardinal got up to speak, he looked over at Bishop Mansell and said: "Don't get too comfortable in that chair, Henry!" The Cathedral exploded with laughter and the one who laughed the hardest was Bishop Mansell.

Before I went to Waterbury for the 100th Anniversary celebration, I learned from Bill Pape that when the original St. Margaret's Church was built in 1910, it was completed in eight weeks, and that the entire cost of building it was $10,295. My mother, my Aunt Nell and all of my uncles, John, Ed, Tom and Den, grew up in that Parish and attended St. Margaret's Grammar School at no cost. And so, I contributed $10,295, the cost of the original church built in 1910, to the Parish on behalf of all of us. As I explained to Father Villa, the pastor of St. Margaret's, it was not a donation but rather a partial payment on a just and long-standing debt. I can't express in words, the enormous joy I have derived from having done that! Try it sometime, you'll like it. Thank God I was able to do it.

This is a picture of my uncles, from left to right, Tom, Ed and Dennis. My Uncle John, the "bookie" from Philadelphia, was unavailable for the picture for reasons never disclosed!

Chapter 3: *The Brooklyn Dodgers and Related Matters*

As I've indicated when Aunt Nell took me in, "Gramp" lived with us and was my best pal.

Waterbury is between New York and Boston. Consequently, almost everyone in Waterbury was either a Yankee fan or to a lesser extent, a Red Sox fan.

For some reason, "Gramp" was a Brooklyn Dodger fan and as a result so was I! To the best of my knowledge, we were the only two Brooklyn Dodger fans in Waterbury.

I used to argue with my friends throughout every summer for hours on end as to whether the Dodgers were better than the Yankees or vice versa. Unfortunately, the Yankees beat the Dodgers in the World Series regularly and the statistical information published in the "Sporting News" heavily favored the Yankees. But I never let those facts bother me. Incidentally, that training served me well when I later became a lawyer!

My uncle, Tom Shanahan, had left Waterbury; went to New York and realized early success as a banker. Every season he would get front row tickets at Ebbets Field to a Dodger game for my grandfather and me. It was the biggest event of the year for both of us!

In those days the seats in the boxes were not bolted into the floor and could be moved. One year I moved my seat right up to the front rail which I grasped with both hands. My forearms were along the protective screen. Joe "Ducky" Medwick hit a foul ball which hit the outside of the protective screen and I was knocked off my seat! Although I was not hurt, Dodger personnel took me down into the Dodger dugout and put me on a training table. Whitlow Wyatt, a twenty-game winner and the "ace" of the Dodgers, rubbed my arm. I was transfixed and I didn't wash that arm for the rest of the summer!

By far the worst tragedy of my boyhood was the death of "Gramp" on December 27, 1941. He was given the Last Rites by Father J. Oliver

Cronin, one of our parish priests. Father Cronin later told us that when my grandfather confessed his sins he said: "All I've done since my last confession was to call the Japs a bunch of bastards." I remember his wake at Mulvilles Funeral Parlor and his funeral mass at St. Margaret's as if they were yesterday. Throughout my entire life, I've always called upon "Gramp" whenever I've had a serious problem and he's never let me down.

We finally got our revenge against the loathed and despised Yankees in 1955 when we beat their ass in a seven game World Series! Johnny Podres, who died recently, won two of the four Dodger victories. My only regret was that "Gramp" wasn't around to see it.

Then came 1957 and total disaster not only for my beloved Brooklyn Dodgers but for the New York Giants and New York City as well! Ebbets Field was in very poor condition and Walter O'Malley, the owner of the Dodgers, wanted a new stadium in Brooklyn.

For reasons best known to himself, Robert Moses, a politically powerful builder of roads, bridges, tunnels, beaches and buildings, insisted that the new stadium be built in Queens.

O'Malley threatened to move the Dodgers to Los Angeles and urged Horace Stoneham, the owner of the New York Giants, to move the Giants who had played at the Polo Grounds in Manhattan since 1883, to San Francisco. If the Giants didn't go to San Francisco, the National League would not have allowed the Dodgers to go to L.A. because it was too far to travel to play one team. O'Malley also had in mind the continuance of the great rivalry between the Brooklyn Dodgers and the New York Giants, which was every bit as fierce as the rivalry between the Dodgers and the Yankees.

Eventually, it became clear that O'Malley would go unless he got a new stadium in Brooklyn. But Moses would not back down and Robert Wagner, the Mayor of New York City at the time, did not have the courage to overrule the powerful Moses, although he obviously had the power to do so!

As a result, New York City lost two magnificent baseball franchises. Thousands of baseball fans were devastated and never recovered. And New York City lost untolled revenues.

But saddest of all, Brooklyn lost its soul and has yet to get it back!

Shame on Moses; more shame on Wagner and I'm not too happy with O'Malley either. I'll get over all of this eventually. I just need a little more time. After all, it's only been 53 years since the Dodgers left Brooklyn.

Incidentally, Mayor Wagner also allowed the demolition of the old Penn Station, an architectural Stanford White masterpiece that should be standing to this day! One positive result of that atrocity was the establishment of the Landmarks Commission of the City of New York.

Before I leave the subject of the Brooklyn Dodgers or the old Penn Station, whichever you prefer, permit me to address a current baseball injustice.

When the Mets came to New York in 1962, I became an instant fan. Simply rooting against the Yankees wasn't sufficiently satisfying — especially when they were winning — I needed a team to root for!

A few years later, I prevailed upon my law firm to take a four seat box at Shea Stadium and subsequently a second four seat box. I can't tell you how many wonderful days and nights I've had at Met Games at Shea with relatives, friends, clients, potential clients, bishops, clergymen, politicians, law partners and associates.

A very important feature of these games is having a couple of cold beers and a "dirty water" hot dog. What is a "dirty water" hot dog you may ask?

There are two kinds of hot dogs that are available at a baseball game. The first is the foot long monster which is cooked interminably on rollers until it develops a casing which is impenetrable and is inedible even if penetrated. They are available only at the stands

The "dirty water" hot dog, on the other hand, is smaller and softer. It is steamed and cooked in boiling dirty water and is delivered in large tin cases by strolling vendors. Don't ask me why the water is "dirty." It just is, and I assume that it adds a little flavor!

At Shea Stadium I knew exactly where the "dirty water" hot dog vendors emerged with their delicacies and I was always first on line.

I'm rambling again, which is fun – but let's get back to the current baseball injustice.

Fred Wilpon, the owner of the New York Mets, built a new stadium, called "Citi Field" which replaced Shea and replicates Ebbets Field in some respects. We have seats at the new stadium and incidentally I am pleased to report that "dirty water" hot dogs are available there as they were at Shea!

Here's the complaint. An enormous amount of taxpayer money went into the building of the new stadium. That being the case, the public at large should be afforded a substantial benefit. Wrong. There are fewer seats for the general public at the new stadium than there were at Shea and they cost much more than they did at Shea. This huge increase in the price of tickets together with the increased costs of accessories such as score cards, popcorn, Cracker Jacks, parking, drinks, food and souvenirs has put the cost of attending a baseball game at the new stadium beyond the reach of the average family. We are not talking about an elitist sport like polo or tennis. We are talking about baseball — the national pastime.

In the meantime, the new stadium is replete with skyboxes leased by organizations which will generate massive revenues for the Met organization.

I know Fred Wilpon a little bit. He's a businessman but he's also a pleasant and decent person and I hope he'll take another look at this situation. How about using some percentage of the skybox profits to lower the cost of general admission seats?

But the real blame lies with the politicians who agreed to governmental financial support to build the new stadium. They should have and could have provided some modicum of protection for the general public and they utterly failed to do so. Shame on them!

While the new stadium replicates Ebbets Field in some respects, it bears the stamp of Jackie Robinson. He is everywhere and justifiably so! He was the greatest Dodger of them all and he played in Brooklyn — not Los Angeles.

When Robinson went on his first road trip with the Dodgers in 1947, he went to Cincinnati, Ohio, to play the "Reds." During pre-game infield practice he was booed mercilessly by the crowd because he was black. "Pee Wee" Reese, the highly revered captain of the Dodgers and a Kentuckian, left his position at shortstop, went over to Robinson, engaged him in conversation and put his arm around his shoulder — the booing stopped instantly.

That moment is memorialized in a bronze sculpture of Reese and Robinson by sculpture William Behrends and stands at KeySpan Park in Brooklyn where the Brooklyn "Cyclones", a Met farm team, play their home games.

Because I had raised money for the sculpture at a fund-raiser at Gracie Mansion, I was invited to join Mayor Bloomberg, Jackie Robinson's wife, Rachael, and others at the unveiling ceremony which took place on November 1, 2005.

On that occasion I asked Mrs. Robinson whether she had been present when "Pee Wee" Reese put his arm around Jackie's shoulder in Cincinnati. She explained that she was not there because at that time teams would not pay for the wives of players to attend "away" games. I then said to her, "In my opinion it was the greatest moment in sports." She smiled at me gently and said: "It was the greatest moment in human relations."

Before leaving the subject of baseball, I have to add another event. On July 20, 2010, I was informed that I had been asked by the Mets to throw out the first ball of the Met game to be played against the Arizona Diamondbacks at Citi Field on Friday, July 30, 2010, at 7:10 PM.

I accepted on the condition that my eleven-year-old grandson, James, be allowed to accompany me to the mound and the Mets agreed.

On the afternoon of the game, I practiced throwing a baseball 60 feet with my friend and law partner, Christine Cesare, in the halls of our law offices.

That night at the game, the Mets took the field following the Star Spangled Banner, and James and I then walked out to the mound together while our names were being announced over the public address system! Despite some modicum of anxiety, I threw a strike and James gave me a "high five." As the Mets catcher, Henry Blanco, came toward us to give us the ball, I said, "Henry, I hope I didn't hurt your hand" and he laughed.

The fact that I am the Chair of Group Health Incorporated and the Vice Chair of Emblem Health, both substantial Met advertisers for many years, may have had a little something to do with my selection. But I prefer to think that it was primarily because the Mets somehow learned about the extraordinary baseball ability I showed when I played shortstop for St. Margaret's Grammar School in Waterbury, Connecticut, during the early 1940s.

This is a picture of James and me on the field at Citi Field on the night I threw out the first ball.

Chapter 4: *Brushes with the Kennedys*

As graduation from St. Margaret's approached, I was looking forward to going to Crosby High School with my friends and then to work at Scoville Manufacturing Company, where my father worked and served as a union shop steward.

Then came the call that changed my life. It was from my Uncle Tom Shanahan, the family patriarch, who had provided us with Dodger tickets and many other kindnesses over the years.

He had been very close to my mother, his sister, and was fond of me. "Jimmy," he said, "as to high school, you have the choice of going to LaSalle Academy, on Long Island, run by the Christian Brothers, or Cranwell Preparatory School in Lenox, Massachusetts, run by the Jesuits. Which one will it be?" I quickly concluded that Cranwell was closer to Waterbury and responded "Uncle Tom, I'll go to Cranwell!"

And so I did, thanks to his enormous generosity. Cranwell was a school for the very, very wealthy. As a matter of fact, I was the only student who arrived by public transportation. Everyone else arrived in a limousine. When I got to be an upperclassman I frequently hitchhiked from Cranwell to Waterbury to save the bus fare, unbeknownst to Aunt Nell or my father. When I think of it now, I shudder!

Among my fellow students was Ted Kennedy. He was among a handful of eighth graders attending Cranwell. My recollection of him was that he was quiet, disengaged and slept a great deal. He left after eighth grade.

As I have indicated, after graduation from Cranwell in 1949, I moved to New York with Aunt Nell, attended Holy Cross College and later Fordham Law School.

In 1952, Congressman Jack Kennedy of Massachusetts ran for the United States Senate against Henry Cabot Lodge, Jr. I was a senior at Holy Cross at the time and because Holy Cross is located in Worcester,

Massachusetts, I had a close-up, day in and day out, view of the campaign. It was the most electrifying political campaign I've ever witnessed. It was fueled and orchestrated by the Patriarch, Joe Kennedy, and virtually everyone in the Kennedy clan campaigned unreservedly on a daily basis. The advertising was massive, unrelenting and covered every city, town and village in the Commonwealth.

When Kennedy defeated Henry Cabot Lodge, Jr., I turned over in my mind again and again — and with considerable satisfaction I might add, the old New England bromide that said: "The Cabots speak only to the Lodges and the Lodges speak only to God." How sweet it was! For me it was the beginning of what would become a lifelong, intense interest in politics and public service.

I thought of Jack Kennedy again in 1956, the year I graduated Fordham Law School, when I read his book entitled *Profiles in Courage* — extolling the virtues of Senators who had acted from conscience — when it was politically damaging to do so — a more common practice then than it is today. At that point, I started to follow his political career closely.

Upon graduation from Fordham Law School I was commissioned as a Second Lieutenant in the Marine Corps; performed the nine months of infantry training mandatory for all Marine Corps officers at the time and was then assigned to legal duties, prosecuting and defending General Courts Martial at Quantico, Virginia. Incidentally, it was a lot easier to prosecute than to defend!

My father died in 1956 while I was in the Marine Corps. He was extremely proud that I was a Marine Corps. officer and I derived satisfaction from attending his wake and funeral mass in uniform. I knew he would love that. As was the case with "Gramp," he was waked at Mulvilles Funeral Parlor and his funeral mass was at St. Margaret's.

He was also proud that I was a lawyer – but to a lesser degree. He had sound values!

Upon my discharge from the Marine Corps, I became an Assistant District Attorney of New York County under the late Frank S. Hogan.

By this time, my Uncle Tom Shanahan had become a very powerful figure in the Democratic Party in New York; friendly with Joe Kennedy and supportive of Joe's efforts to make his son, Jack, President of the United States. In 1960, he suggested that I get involved in the Kennedy presidential campaign against Richard Nixon and I did, after work, whenever I could.

On the night of November 7, 1960, Jack Kennedy appeared at a rally at the New York Coliseum. I was there and met him to my great delight. The next day, I learned to my surprise that after he left the Coliseum, he went to Waterbury, Connecticut — my hometown! The people of Waterbury had waited for him on Waterbury's "green" until 3:00 A.M. It was his last campaign stop and the next day he was elected President of the United States.

The deciding state in that presidential election was Illinois. Cook County which embraced Chicago, ruled by Mayor Richard Daley, did not report its final results until 4:00 A.M. I stayed tuned to the bloody end and went to bed a happy man.

Skeptics claim that Daley had held out until he had determined how many votes Jack needed from Cook County to carry the State. Others joked that Joe Kennedy had told Daley that although Daley was to assure Jack's victory he, Joe, wasn't going to pay for a landslide!

In 1962, Ted Kennedy ran for the Senate in Massachusetts and won. My Uncle Tom had a fund-raiser for him at the "21" Club which I attended.

In the early part of 1963, my uncle suggested that I consider moving to Washington and becoming involved with the Kennedys. I loved New York and didn't want to move. But my Uncle made an appointment for me to meet with the newly elected Senator Ted Kennedy and I agreed to go.

Before my meeting with Senator Kennedy, my Uncle was in a very serious automobile accident on the Westside Highway and critically injured. He had been under intensive care at Downtown Hospital for some time before I went to Washington for my meeting with Senator Kennedy.

When I walked into Senator Kennedy's office at about 10:30 in the morning, we exchanged greetings and he added "I'm sorry about your Uncle Tom." I said "What are you talking about?" He said, "He died earlier this morning." I fell to pieces and he graciously left me alone in his office. After I finally pulled myself together, I emerged from his office and he asked if there was anything he could do. I told him I was going to fly back to New York right away and he had his driver drive me to the airport.

I was grateful to him for his kindness on that occasion and never forgot it. But I never went back. Approximately nine months later he would suffer the tragic loss of his beloved brother, Jack.

Everyone remembers where they were on Friday, November 22, 1963, when they learned that President Kennedy had been shot in Dallas, Texas.

I was working for Frank Hogan and was having a late lunch with some colleagues at Forlini's Restaurant on Baxter Street close by the D.A.'s office. I was thunderstruck as was all of America! I went home and watched television continuously for the next 48 hours without sleep. It was horrible and grew worse as the story unfolded. I watched the same footage again and again and again and fought off tears. It was grotesquely addictive because of its magnitude, the depths and reach of the pain that it inflicted, the extreme worry that it generated nationally and the myriad questions that it raised.

Bobby Kennedy was President Kennedy's Attorney General and his closest advisor. After his brother's assassination, he resigned as Attorney General and in 1964 successfully ran against Kenneth Keating for the U.S. Senate in New York.

By that time, I had left the D.A.'s office and joined the law firm that I've been with for the past 45 years, Robinson Silverman & Pearce (now Bryan Cave). Consequently, I was in a position to participate in Bobby's campaign heavily, and I did.

As a person, I believe that Bobby was the best of the brood. He genuinely cared for the poor and the downtrodden — and worked assiduously to better their lot — not simply because of politics but because he loved them deeply and truly.

He was a friend to and a stalwart supporter of the great labor leader Cesar Chavez, whom I admired tremendously and worked for pro bono, during his country-wide boycott of Gallo wine, grapes and lettuce. The Farm Workers knew how to put up a picket line which was rarely crossed and if so at some risk. Nowadays picket lines in New York City consist of a blow up of a rat which is not very compelling! Back to the Kennedys.

In 1966, my family and I were living in Stuyvesant Town on the East Side of Manhattan and Orin Lehman was running for Congress in that District. Senator Bobby Kennedy was campaigning with Lehman and they did a "drop in" at our apartment. This is a picture of that "drop in" which appeared in the local paper.

As you can see, my wife Jackie, was somewhat taken aback. My daughter, Rose, the beautiful little girl in the picture is now the very highly regarded Commissioner of Investigations of the City of New York! The other child in the picture is my son, Dennis.

When Bobby was assassinated in 1968, Ted delivered his eulogy at St. Patrick's Cathedral and I was there. It was the most moving eulogy I've ever heard. As he drew toward the end he said: "My brother need not be idealized, or enlarged in death beyond what he was in life, to be remembered simply as a good and decent man, who saw wrong and tried to right it, saw suffering and tried to heal it, saw war and tried to stop it."

And with a quaking voice he ended with a quote from Bobby:

"Some men see things as they are and say why. I dream things that never were and say why not."

My contacts with the Kennedys have continued. I know Bobby's son, Joe Kennedy, and Ted's son, Patrick, and I supported both of them in their Congressional campaigns.

I worked with John F. Kennedy, Jr. when he was in Mayor Koch's administration. When he was considering law school, I urged him to go to Fordham and arranged for him to take a tour of the law school with Dean John Feerick. Although accepted by Fordham, he finally decided to attend N.Y.U. Law School — a serious mistake.

Sometime thereafter, John Jr. went to work for Bob Morgenthau, the District Attorney of New York County – my old office. After he had been there a short period, I attended a dinner at Ed Koch's apartment and Jacqueline Onassis Kennedy was a guest as was her escort – Maurice Tempelsman – the enormously wealthy owner of diamond mines.

I had the opportunity to give her the extraordinary history of the office of the District Attorney of New York County during the days of Tom Dewey, Frank Hogan and Bob Morgenthau. She was delighted that her son had gone to work there.

She was very soft spoken, laid back and, indeed, shy in a certain way – but at the same time extraordinarily charming.

Several years ago I received a telephone call from Robert F. Kennedy, Jr. asking for a meeting in my capacity as the Chair of the Doris Duke Charitable Foundation. We met at my office and he requested that the Foundation consider a grant to his "River Keeper" organization which is devoted in large measure to the environmental protection of the Hudson River. Although we were not able to grant his request it was pleasing to see him heavily involved in important business.

The death of Ted Kennedy raises the question of who will assume leadership of the Kennedy clan. I don't have any idea as to who will assume that role, if anyone. What I do know is that the so-called Kennedy Era is not over and that we will see the Kennedys in leadership roles for many years to come. They are a very large group of very talented and devoted people.

As I've said, I learned the importance and value of unionism at the feet of my father.

It is axiomatic that one worker has no strength whatever to deal with an employer as to wages, working conditions and benefits, one on one. That boss is in complete control and that worker has no leverage whatever.

As stated, when I left the office of District Attorney Frank Hogan, I went to work for the law firm of Robinson Silverman and Pearce (now Bryan Cave) and my primary job was to represent unions and their related funds. It was for that very reason that I joined that firm and because I knew that my father (by then deceased) would be pleased. He had paid my board and tuition at Holy Cross College and my tuition at Fordham Law School out of hard-earned wages and at great personal sacrifice. Whenever I received my grades, he posted them on the union bulletin board. I knew that. It was a very strong incentive and I responded accordingly.

In all the years I represented the United Furniture Workers of America, I never came across an employer who wasn't convinced that he was being more than generous with his employees. Everyone of them was shocked when their employees sought union representation, especially in states like Mississippi, South Carolina, North Carolina and Tennessee. And, invariably, they fought to the death to ward it off. Incidentally, the Furniture Workers in their day knew how to put up a picket line every bit as well as the Farm Workers. I walked those picket lines when the Furniture Workers struck the American Tent Company at Canton, Mississippi, in 1968 and again when they struck the Lazy Boy Chair Company at Florence, South Carolina, in 1991.

At the time of the strike, the workers at the American Tent Company were receiving the minimum wage and nothing else. I'm proud to tell you that the Furniture Workers won first contracts at both companies and as I've said, I derived enormous satisfaction from representing the United Farm Workers pro bono when Cesar Chavez conducted their national boycott of Gallo wine, grapes and lettuce.

This is a picture of a young Jim Gill address-ing an annual convention of the United Furniture Workers of America in Memphis, Tennessee.

Unless workers are united, represented collectively and have the wherewithal to close down a shop, they are at the whim and caprice of the employer. The right to organize and have collective representation and the right to strike are essential. Although those rights are embodied in the law, they have been diluted in large measure over the years by unscrupulous employers, the National Labor Relations Board and our courts. Incidentally unions can be helpful to employers in many ways where sound labor relationships exist.

Have there been abuses by certain unions and certain labor leaders? No question. Jimmy Hoffa, of course, is the prime example — strong-arm tactics, threats, intimidation and the looting of union funds and pension funds. What's even more shocking is the fact that there were times when Hoffa's membership actually accepted that kind of conduct because Hoffa was doing well by them! And there have been other union abuses and excesses as well, including some by unions representing governmental employees.

But those who have defamed or embarrassed the labor movement make up a very small percentage of the organized labor force. Unfortunately, they are the only ones you hear about in the media. The hardworking, decent, honorable labor leaders, who devote a lifetime to obtaining living wages, decent working conditions and basic benefits for their members are unsung and receive little or no attention.

The labor movement is a magnificent cause. It is the way in which workers can gain a larger share of prosperity, move up the ladder, educate their children and see them and their grandchildren go on to greater heights.

It bothers me greatly that young people don't seem to recognize the importance of the labor movement and do not support it! God knows they get involved in a host of far lesser causes but not the labor movement which is so important to the advancement of such a large portion of our society.

One of my great professional joys has been working closely on labor matters with three young lawyers, the late Mike O'Toole, Andy Irving and Kyle Flaherty, all of whom became dear friends over my past 45 years plus with the firm.

Another thing that baffles me is the antipathy that seems to exist between labor and the Catholic Church. Philosophically, that should not be. Catholic teaching promotes the basic principles of the labor movement.

Quadragesimo Anno and Rerum Novarum, both encyclicals of the Church, specifically refer to and espouse the right to a living wage, the right to organize and the right to strike!

I'm pleased to say that the Feerick Center at Fordham Law School is engaged in an effort to ameliorate the situation. His Excellency William Murphy, the Bishop of Rockville Center, John Sweeney, the Former President of the AFL and Dennis Rivera, of the Hospital Workers, have produced a document in that connection which hopefully will be the blueprint for labor relations between the Church and organized labor going forward. I know all of those involved and I am certain that they will make meaningful strides to attain that goal.

Friendships are very special. Family relationships are, of course, primary. But non-family friendships are free and clear of prefixed entanglements. They are free of solemn vows or legal or blood obligations that exist as in the case of a spouse, a child or other relatives.

You choose your friends without regard to other duties or obligations and because you enjoy them and their company. If problems arise, there are few complications and minimal harm. That's why true friendships are so precious and why I value my friendships so dearly.

One of my dearest friends was the late Cardinal John O'Connor who I met at a dinner party at Ed Koch's apartment. We had much in common and hit it off from the very start.

Our fathers were both union members and believers in the union movement; the Cardinal was the chaplain for the Second Marine Division and later a two star admiral in charge of all military chaplains; I was a Marine Corps legal officer; we each enjoyed the other's sense of humor and we were in tune politically.

In 1992 the Cardinal asked me to be the honoree and principal speaker at the Friendly Sons of St. Patrick annual dinner on March 17. The Friendly Sons organization is 226 years old and the annual dinner is one of the two best dinners of the year in New York City, the other being the Al Smith dinner. Approximately 2,500 men attend the Friendly Sons dinner and they are as tough a crowd as any speaker can ever face. They want to be entertained and not lectured and woe to the speaker who fails to do so.

Fortunately my speech went over well and especially with Cardinal O'Connor. A copy of that speech is attached as Appendix B for those who may be interested. Many say it's my best.

Several months later he asked me to serve as general counsel to the Board of Trustees of St. Patrick' Cathedral which he chaired and I have continued in that capacity under Cardinal Egan and now under Archbishop Timothy Dolan – also friends. In addition, Cardinal O'Connor inducted me into the Knights of Malta.

This is a picture of Cardinal O'Connor, my wife Jackie and me.

Cardinal O'Connor was also very close to my dear friend, Ed Koch, the subject of my next chapter. During their relationship, Ed who is of the Jewish faith, attended mass at St. Patrick's with amazing frequency.

On one such occasion, Cardinal O'Connor intoned: "Now that Mayor Koch is comfortably seated in the front row – let the mass begin."

On another such occasion, he announced: "For the benefit of the non-Catholics with us today, if you don't know when to stand, sit or kneel, simply follow the lead of Mayor Koch who is seated in the front row."

Another dear friend is Al D'Amato and by happenstance my friendship with him is also related to the Friendly Sons annual dinner.

In 1985, Al was asked to be the honoree and principal speaker at the dinner and he was frightened to death. I knew him slightly and he, acting on the advise of others, asked me to write his speech for him which I agreed to do on three conditions:

1. He couldn't change a word;

2. He had to spend St. Patrick's day with me rehearsing his delivery; and

3. No drinking until after the speech was delivered.

He agreed to my conditions. I wrote the speech and he was a sensation. After that we became the best of friends.

He's a true friend. When trouble comes – he's there. Not just with words but with everything he's got. He's exceptionally bright which many don't realize until its too late and he's the most adroit political analyst I've ever known. During his 18 years in the United States Senate he was unabashedly "pro-life" on abortion although it cost him politically.

For years I've been urging him to hire someone to catalogue all of the things that he did while in the Senate. If he were to do so, he would undoubtedly emerge as the most effective senator New York has ever produced and yet he has still to do so. I think that the reason for that omission is the fact that he is always looking forward and rarely looks back.

I also count former New York State Governor George Pataki among my friends. He appointed me as Acting Director of the Governor's Office of Employee Relations, Chair of the Long Island Power Authority and Chair of Battery Park City Authority. I served in each of those posts pro bono and with great pleasure and satisfaction.

This is a picture of former U.S. Senator Al D'Amato, former New York State Governor George Pataki and me.

I've urged another friend, Bob Morgenthau, the former District Attorney of New York County, to write his life story and he, like Al D'Amato, also declined because he never looks back. My friendship with Bob goes back to his election as District Attorney of New York County in 1975, which took place shortly after the death of Frank Hogan. I was deeply involved in Bob's campaign in 1975 and every one thereafter. He served as District Attorney for 34 years and indeed is an icon.

Shortly after his election in 1975 he asked me to form the Hogan-Morgenthau Associates and I did so. I've served as its chair ever since. Our annual dinner is a huge reunion for all past and present assistants.

Before leaving this chapter, I must mention my oldest friend, the late Paul Curran who died on September 4, 2008. I could write reams about Paul Curran, the public servant, the lawyer, the Catholic layman, the husband, the father, the grandfather, the man and the friend. But I will simply say that we grew up together; and we grew old together and he was just the best in all categories.

The rest of my friends know who they are and they will all be pallbearers at my funeral mass!

I met Ed Koch through our mutual friend, the late Allen Schwartz who later became Ed's Corporation Counsel. Allen and I had become friends when we both served as Assistant District Attorneys of New York County under Frank Hogan.

When Allen left Hogan's office, he joined Ed's law firm as a partner. He introduced me to Ed in 1973 when Ed ran for Mayor of New York City for the first time. I supported Ed in that brief and unsuccessful campaign and in all of his mayoral campaigns thereafter.

In 1988 Mayor Ed Koch appointed me as chair of the Joint Commission on Integrity in the Public Schools and we worked together for more than a year. The work of that Commission is discussed in the next chapter.

I also served as a member of Ed's Judicial Screening Panel throughout his mayoralty.

I brought Ed Koch into our law firm when he left the mayoralty in 1990 and he's been with us ever since. On January 8, 1990, I participated in a roast of Ed at the New York City Bar Association. My remarks included the following:

"My job tonight is to defend Ed Koch. It's my understanding, however, that my defense of Ed is supposed to be much like the defense that Johnny Addy interposed on behalf of Gladys Gooding many years ago at Madison Square Garden when it was located at 50th Street.

At that time Johnny Addy was the ring announcer at Madison Square Garden and on that occasion he entered the ring to announce the main event. He rang the bell several times for attention and a hush fell over the Garden. Addy then announced: 'Gladys Gooding will now sing and play the National Anthem.' At that point a drunk in the balcony got up and shouted out at the top of his lungs: 'Gladys Gooding is a no good God damn whore.' To which Johnny Addy responded: 'Nonetheless,'

Well, I have no intention of interposing a 'Johnny Addy' defense on behalf of Ed. Ed is my friend and partner and I intend to defend him to the hilt.

Many of the charges leveled against Ed are grossly exaggerated and enormously overblown.

Take for instance the allegation that Ed has been intemperate and overly self-indulgent in his attacks upon persons with whom he disagrees or whom he dislikes.

Now I know that Ed referred to Leona Helmsley as the 'Wicked Witch of the West' and the 'Queen of Mean.'

And there's no denying the fact that he called Jimmy Breslin a 'bumble brain and a jerk.'

And I will admit that he labeled Ruth Messinger an 'ideologue and a bomb-thrower.'

And, yes, he referred to Yasser Arafat as an 'international hoodlum.'

And its common knowledge that he called Bella Abzug a 'loud mouth!'

And we all know that he called Jay Goldin a 'snake in the grass.'

And I'm aware that he called Carole Bellamy a 'dingbat' and

Jerry Ford an 'empty suit.'

And yes, it's widely known that he called Jesse Jackson an 'anti-Semite' and Imelda Marcos a 'crook.'

And no one need remind me that he called Kurt Waldheim a 'Nazi pig'; Kadafy a 'weirdo' and Ronald Lauder a 'clown.'

Gary Hart a 'turkey' and Donald Trump a 'hot dog'.

And, obviously I will concede that he called Jack Newfield a 'hump.'

Dan Quayle a 'numb nut' and Nancy Reagan a 'Barbie doll.'

Nonetheless that's about it!

I mean what's the big deal here?

Moreover I would point out that during all of his years in public office, Ed never said a single unkind word about Mother Theresa despite the fact that she was constantly on his nerves."

More than twenty years have gone by since that roast. Throughout that time, Ed's office has been next to mine and we talk every day. We go to lunch together at least three times a week and to countless functions and events. I know the man and his incredible record of achievements as well as anyone. But this is not the place to extol Ed's virtues and accomplishments. Nor is it necessary since he has already done that in the ten books he's written about himself!

And so I will limit myself to several incidents which I find highly entertaining. The first took place when he successfully ran for Mayor in 1977. Ed still has all of the suits he ever purchased, many of which go back to the 50's. Not only does he own them, he actually wears them. And so during the campaign, David Garth, Ed's campaign manager, strongly urged him to go to Dunhill's to buy a couple of new suits. Ed did so — and after trying one of them on, inquired as to its cost. "$1,400" replied the salesman, to which Koch responded: "Get it off of me — get it off me now" — and he ran out of the store!

The next took place shortly after Ed joined our firm and had moved into an apartment on lower 5th Avenue. It was a Monday morning and after we had arrived at work, he told me the following:

"Saturday morning I was walking down 9th Street on the way to Balducci's to buy some provisions when a lovely woman and some of her friends approached me and said 'Mayor, we need you back — you've got to run again' — my answer was: 'No, the people threw me out — and now the people must be punished!'" (That soon became and remains his standard answer when confronted with that kind of exaltation, which occurs almost every day.)

The Mayor went on to say: "But then as I drew close to Balducci's I saw a scruffy looking guy on a bicycle who shouted out 'Hey Koch, you were a shitty Mayor' to which I responded: 'Fuck You!' — You have no idea how good that made me feel."

After Ed had a stroke in 1987, he was recuperating at Gracie Mansion and was visited by Mother Teresa and several of her nuns. It was a hot summer day and while they sat on the porch, Ed offered them lemonade and chocolate chip cookies.

Mother Teresa politely declined explaining that they had a strict rule of never accepting anything from anyone on any of their visits, because if they were to do so in India, poor Indian families would give them food which they needed for their own survival. She went on to explain that the blanket rule allowed them to decline without insulting anyone.

Despite all of that, Ed kept insisting that they try the chocolate chip cookies — proclaiming them to be "the best ever baked."

Finally, as Mother Teresa and her companions were leaving, Ed gave it one more shot — "Mother, you've got to try these chocolate chip cookies — they are world famous and my chef is going to be terribly disappointed" to which Mother Teresa responded: "Wrap 'em up."

Ed is very proud of his record of accomplishments and never fails to defend himself in writing — whenever he comes under attack.

My favorite retort went like this:

"Dear Madam:

You are entitled to your opinion of me and I am entitled to my opinion of you.

My opinion of you is that you are a fool!

All the best."

Ed.

For Ed, every day is an all out crusade, from beginning to end, to remain relevant and involved – and every day he wins! I have never witnessed the kind of unrelenting determination, drive and devotion that he brings to bear on a daily basis.

This is Ed Koch marching in the St. Patrick's Day Parade with Governor George Pataki and others including me on his immediate right. Every year he 'steals' the parade when he throws his arms in the air and shrieks out "It's me" as shown in this picture.

On Wednesday, December 8, 2010, Mayor Bloomberg hosted a party at Gracie Mansion for Ed Koch to celebrate his 86th birthday.

Over 200 people attended including many who served in his administration when he was mayor. It's an annual event and as always it was a great joy.

But the great highlight of this birthday came when Mayor Bloomberg announced that the Queensboro Bridge at 59th Street, which connects Manhattan and Queens, was to be renamed for Ed Koch! A huge sign setting forth the new name of the bridge was unveiled and it was a wonderful moment not only for Ed but for all of us in attendance.

After Ed expressed his gratitude, he quoted from the Great Gatsby by F. Scott Fitzgerald. The quote was from a friend of the Great Gatsby when they were driving across the Queensboro Bridge on their way from Long Island to Manhattan.

"The City seen from the Queensboro Bridge is always the City seen for the first time, in its first wild promise of all the mystery and all the beauty in the world."

Ed then added:

"Nobody else has a bridge like that – only me."

Later he vowed that he would always bring to bear all of his power and influence to keep the bridge free and clear of tolls!

Over the next several days, I reflected on the great generosity of Mayor Bloomberg in naming the 59th Street Bridge for Ed and finally decided to write him a letter in that regard.

It read as follows:

"Dear Mayor:

When history judges mayors of the City of New York, they will be measured to a considerable extent against their peers. That is why your naming of the 59th Street Bridge for Ed Koch was an act of enormous generosity. In doing so, you justifiably lifted Ed up in a wonderful way.

But that act also lifted you up, in that it demonstrated the extraordinarily unselfish and gracious nature of your soul. Hurrah for you and Merry Christmas!"

The key to success for someone not "born to the purple" is education. I came from modest circumstances. But thanks to a loving uncle and father, I received an excellent education. Whatever I've accomplished is the direct result of that education. There is no other way! And for me, it was great fun.

In December of 1988, Mayor Koch, appointed me as Chairman of the Joint Commission on Integrity in the Public Schools. The job of the Commission, which soon became known as the "Gill Commission," was to deal with corruption and inefficiency in the New York City Public School System. It was like "shooting fish in a barrel" and we were in the media regularly. Our staff, headed by my friend and now law partner Austin Campriello, and aided greatly by my friend Jennifer Cunningham, did a spectacular job which resulted in meaningful changes.

This was taken after Ed had sworn me in and we were taking questions from the media.

As a result of our investigation, the totally ineffective office of the Inspector General of the Board of Education was abolished and replaced by an independent Commissioner of Investigations who reports only to the New York City Commissioner of Investigations. That post is currently held by Richard Condon, the former Police Commissioner of The City of New York. As indicated earlier, the position of New York City Commissioner of Investigations is currently held by my daughter, Rose Gill Hearn.

This is my daughter Rose greeting His Holiness Pope Benedict XV when he visited New York City on April 19, 2008.

Another far-reaching change was the elimination of the Community School Boards which we exposed as nothing more than patronage mills. In large measure that was the result of the courageous efforts of Colman Genn, the Superintendent of District 27 in Queens, who surreptitiously recorded conversations with School Board members and later appeared in a segment on *60 Minutes*.

During those days, I had an opportunity to take a very close look at the New York City School System in its entirety and I was appalled. There was no accountability at the top and accordingly none throughout the entire system. At that time, the Board of Education consisted of seven members. Two were appointed by the Mayor and each of the five borough Presidents appointed one. As a result, no one was responsible and there was no commonality of purpose. We recommended that the Legislature empower the Mayor to appoint a majority of the members. While almost everyone agreed that such legislation was desirable, it did not happen until the arrival of Mayor Bloomberg. He had the courage to assume that responsibility and he got it.

The other distressing feature of the system was the abysmal quality of the education and the absence of any effort to improve it. Thousands of children were being flushed through the system and were emerging without being able to read or write! Our Commission surreptitiously placed young looking police officers from the NYPD Intelligence Division into classrooms as students. They not only verified a pathetic teaching level but reported a complete breakdown of discipline as well!

There are some fine schools in the public school system in New York City but they are few and far between. Moreover, getting a child into one is a formidable and often hopeless task.

While Mayor Bloomberg has made substantial progress in improving the City's school system in the face of stiff opposition from the teachers' union, most schools still fall well short of the mark.

For many, the only realistic alternative is a private school. The cost of such schools in New York City is often beyond even upper middle income families. What then? People have been, and are continuing, to move out of New York City in order to get sound, affordable education for their children. That remains the number one priority of many parents and often results in moving elsewhere.

There is nothing more important in society than insuring a sound, comprehensive, ethically based public educational system. Charter schools can make a substantial contribution to that effort as can increased governmental assistance to non-public schools.

There are children with special needs and they must be served; there are children who are intellectually challenged and they must be helped; there are children with behavioral problems and their problems must be addressed. And then there are children who are intellectually superior and they must be afforded an opportunity to realize their full potential.

I'm aware that such an all embracing program is costly, but each of these groups of children must be treated separately. To lump them into one pot is a mistake and detrimental to all of them. These differences have existed from time immemorial and will continue to exist.

Fortunately, there are several schools in the public school system which reach out for the best talent available in terms of students, teachers and administrators in an all-out effort to attain excellence for its own sake. Such schools allow our most gifted youngsters an opportunity to realize their full potential and should be encouraged because it is in the best interests of society to do so. There are other aspects to a well-rounded education including diversity, which should be sought after as well — but not at the expense of excellence.

Students at schools of excellence should be admitted on the basis of scholastic ability only and without regard to color, creed, ethnicity, gender or any other non-scholastic factor. The adoption of any kind of quota to favor any group of students in the admissions process, dilutes quality and diminishes excellence. Some schools which purport to be schools of excellence have even revised their curriculum to accommodate lesser qualified students! That is complete surrender!

This is a picture of me questioning a witness at a public hearing. Next to me is Joe Comperiarti, the Director of Investigations, and next to him is John O'Rourke, a special investigator.

The stark reality of life is that some people are more gifted than others and no particular group of any type or description has a monopoly on talent or the lack thereof.

Accordingly, standards should be set for all scholastic gradations with a view towards bringing out the best in everyone. Lowering standards across the board with the hope of making people feel better and "social passing" are the harbingers of academic failure and social disaster.

By the way, the needs of children should come first and the needs of teachers, second; not the other way around. The notion of incompetent teachers getting paid for doing nothing is horrendous and reminiscent of the days when excess typesetters at newspapers in New York City got paid for sitting around and playing cards.

On the other hand, teaching is a very high calling and good teachers should be honored, respected and compensated more appropriately.

Performance on the part of a teacher's pupils most assuredly should be taken into account in determining teacher compensation. In that connection, there is no substitute for testing in measuring student performance.

Recently, there has been extensive public discussion about the application of the "last in, first out" rule with respect to laying off teachers.

The "last in, first out" rule of organized labor is an old and sacred tenant and justifiably so.

Employees who are employed for longer periods of time have often made sacrifices and contributions to the establishment of collective bargaining rights and the procurement of wages and benefits. More recent employees are the beneficiaries of their efforts.

Accordingly, when layoffs come, those sacrifices and contributions should be recognized and properly so. However, that principle is based upon the assumption that all employees are equally qualified to do the job, e.g., assembly line employees.

It does not apply to employees like teachers, where talents, ability, capacity, scope, dedication and devotion vary enormously.

Teaching is not an assembly line task and students must come first.

Boswell, the biographer of the literary giant Ben Johnson, wrote of an incident wherein Johnson backed a young woman into a corner in a pub in which he had been drinking for an extended period of time. 'Mr. Johnson,' said the young woman, 'you smell' to which Johnson replied: 'Young lady, I don't smell — you smell — I stink.'"

Mrs. Astor once said to Winston Churchill: "Mr. Prime Minister: If I were married to you, I would put poison in your coffee." To which he responded: "Madam, if I were married to you, I would drink it."

Churchill was walking down the aisle of the Parliament when he was approached by an aide who said: "Mr. Prime Minister, your fly is unbuttoned," to which Churchill replied: "Fear not, the dead bird never leaves the nest."

A beautiful model approached Churchill and urged that they have a child together. "Imagine a child with my looks and your brains." Churchill's response: "An enticing proposition indeed — but my concern is a child with my looks and your brains."

George Bernard Shaw sent Churchill two tickets to the opening of a new play saying, "The second ticket is for a friend, if you have one." Churchill answered: "Unable to attend the opening of your new show but will attend the second performance if there is one!"

I've read a great deal of history about Winston Churchill. I think that he was the greatest leader of the 20th Century. Unlike many others, he was on to Hitler from the very beginning and Stalin as well. He contributed more to the defeat of Nazi Germany than any other person and was in the forefront of the effort to contain the Soviet Union.

Despite all of that, he was summarily removed from office in an election, immediately after the end of the war.

Several years ago at an Al Smith dinner, I sat on the dais with the former Prime Minister of England, Tony Blair, who was the honoree and I had an opportunity to talk with him as to why Churchill had been so mistreated when he had done so much. His answer was that the English had been in the thick of the war for 8 long years; were "dreadfully weary" of it and associated Churchill with that war. It makes sense and is the best explanation I've heard.

David McCulloch is one of the great historians of our time and I've read all of his books including, *Truman, John Adams, Mornings on Horseback* and *1776*. Over the years, I've met and talked with him at the "21" Club and the Yale Club, my two favourite hangouts.

On one such occasion a rather obnoxious character in an obvious effort to demonstrate his vast store of knowledge commended McCulloch on his treatment of the "ABC affair" in John Adams to which David responded: "I believe you're referring to the 'XYZ affair.' Incidentally ABC is a television network." It was delicious!

I wrote to David asking for permission to use that story in this book. He wrote back and said, "I don't remember the story but print it anyway!" He then went on to say that he had been lecturing on the coast and that during a question and answer period was asked, "Mr. McCulloch, what other presidents have you interviewed besides Harry Truman and John Adams?" He told me I could use that one too.

One of the finest and most hilarious public speakers of my time was William Hughes Mulligan.

Mulligan taught at Fordham Law School for 25 years and when I attended Fordham Law School, I took every course he taught. He later became dean of our Law School and subsequently was appointed to the United States District Court of Appeals for the Second Circuit.

Not surprisingly, his most well known speech was delivered at an annual dinner of the Friendly Sons of St. Patrick held on March 17, 1972, during which he espoused the proposition that Christopher Columbus was not an Italian but rather an Irishman by the name of Lynch. His authority was Samuel Eliot Morison's book, *Admiral of the Ocean Sea*. This is what he said:

"Morison's book gives a physical description of Columbus which was provided by his own contemporaries; I quote pages 40-41:

'He was more than middling tall, aquiline nose, blue eyes, complexion light and tending to bright red, beard and hair red. When he was angry he would exclaim 'May God take you.' In matter of religion he was so strict that for fasting and saying all the canonical offices he might have been taken for a member of a religious order.'

Gentlemen, in all honesty and frankness, how many religious, blue-eyed, red-faced, red-haired Italians have you met in your life? Friendly Sons and Friends, not only am I suggesting but I think the facts clearly establish that in reality Columbus was Lynch, or Lynch was Columbus, whichever way you want it."

When Mulligan delivered his speech to the Friendly Sons of St. Patrick on March 16, 1979, he was a judge of the United States Court of Appeals for the Second Circuit. He began his speech as follows:

"It is indeed an honor to respond to the toast to the United States. I bring to you all the felicitations and best wishes of the United States Court of Appeals for the Second Circuit — five judges concurred — three dissented — and one judge concurred in part and dissented in part. He would felicitate but thought that 'best wishes' was too effusive."

When he addressed the St. John's University law Alumni Association on December 5, 1981, he had just resigned from the Second Circuit Court of Appeals and offered the following explanation for having done so:

"One of the prerequisites of a federal judge is the right to use an official plate – U.S.J. followed by a numeral. When I joined the court in 1971,

I was U.S.J. 52; six years later I was U.S.J. 27; in 1979 I was U.S.J. 22. The declining number was dependent upon my seniority. Since judges seldom, if ever, resigned, the declining number actually reflected the death rate of my colleagues. Every year I received an annual intimation of my own mortality, and it was quite disquieting. I gave the statistics to a doctor friend of mine and after careful study he reported to me that the license plate statistics were as accurate a mortality table as any he had encountered. I asked him what his advice was – instead of orange juice, aspirin, and bed rest, he told me that when I got down to U.S.J. 5, I should sell my car. He didn't claim that this would make me immortal, but he did say that the declining plate number undoubtedly expedited the aging process of the judiciary and was psychologically debilitating. In 1981 I reached the age of 63 and also received a new plate-U.S.J. 7. The effect was somewhat traumatic: in seven years I would reach the biblical term of three score and ten, and U.S.J. 1. The message was clear and compelling. Rather than sell the car, I decided to quit the bench and get back to a three-digit number which will, I hope, ensure me of a greater life expectancy. I realize this was a rather drastic remedy and did not mention to the press the real reason for my decision to leave the bench. I trust you will keep it in the confidence of this room."

How does one become a Democrat, a Republican, an Independent, a Liberal, a Conservative or whatever?

A lot of ingredients go into the mix. Were you raised in modest circumstances or where you born to the purple? Did you grow up in an apartment in a ghetto? Did you live in a three-family house in an ethnic neighborhood or did you live in a one-family house in upscale surroundings? Did your father wear a suit and tie to work or work clothes? Did you grow up in a closely knit family? What kind of teaching and training did you receive from those who raised you? How were you treated when you were growing up?

Where did you go to grammar school and high school? Did you finish? Did you go to college? What did you study?

Did you receive religious training? If so, what kind? Were there experiences and encounters that shaped your thinking, peaked your interest or turned you off?

Were your parents registered with a political party? If so, which one? For whom did they vote? Have siblings and friends influenced you and if so, how?

What newspapers do you read? To what radio programs do you listen? What TV shows do you watch? What books have you read? Have you been exposed to people who differ from you racially, ethnically and religiously? Do you belong to clubs or associations? If so, which ones and why?

What do you do for a living? What are your ambitions? Who are your heroes? What do you do for fun?

From all of that background and a great deal more, philosophical leanings, tendencies and beliefs, emerge which in turn often form the basis of a political affiliation.

It is impossible to put reasonable people into an absolute 100%

"political box," because they just don't fit. Yet many foolishly attempt to do so!

I'll offer myself as an example. I came from a modest means and accordingly feel that Government has an obligation to the poor. With the abundance of food with which we are blessed in this country, no one should die of starvation, suffer from malnutrition or indeed go to bed hungry. Similarly, everyone ought to have basic and fundamental medical coverage and affordable housing. On the other hand the staggering cost of those benefits and others as well must be kept under fiscal control which has not been the case. (Serious worries and concerns about the viability of Social Security benefits have been raised recently.)

Recipients of welfare benefits should be presumed to be worthy recipients in need and should not be denigrated or disparaged because of their needs. On the other hand, those who refuse available employment should be cut off and those who "game the system" should be punished.

My father was a lifelong member of the Machinist Workers Union and I'm pro-union. Yet, I'm aware of and rail against union excesses and abuses because they hurt unionism and working persons so severely. Such excesses by some printing and longshoremen unions led to the destruction of those industries in New York City and the loss of thousands of well-paying jobs!

I was born and raised a Catholic and attended Catholic schools. Accordingly, I believe in Catholic principles and the rights of all religious groups. I am not kindly disposed to atheists, however, who work to stamp out the religious rights of others who believe in God.

I served in the U.S. Marine Corps. I'm proud of that affiliation and I'm supportive of our military establishments. But I've lived through war after war and regard it as the greatest evil on earth. Such action should only be taken when there is a just cause and no other reasonable alternative; its object is clearly defined and there is a reasonable prospect of success within a reasonable period of time.

I served as an Assistant District Attorney of New York County and appreciate the importance of law enforcement. On the other hand, I think it's appalling that people serving time in our prisons are often mistreated and abused by other inmates who control those prisons with the knowledge and consent of prison guards. It's a recognized but accepted wrong which few care about because the victims are prisoners. Moreover, in my opinion, conditions in many youth jails are deplorable and counter productive to the best interests of society. Incidentally, I've been a member of the New York State Board of Prisoner Legal Services since 1993. Finally I am aware that some in law enforcement abuse their vast powers outrageously and visit egregious wrongs upon innocent victims.

I'm a lawyer and fully appreciate the importance of the rule of law as the difference between an ordered society and the jungle. Yet I recognize the right to demonstrate in an orderly and peaceful manner to change the law or foster governmental action.

I got to where I am because of education and so I treasure education as the way out of poverty and the way up the ladder. Still, I am outraged by the failure of so many educators and unions to serve our children well and properly in this all important area.

I have been exposed to all kinds of human beings over many years and despise discrimination which is a non-thinking blanket condemnation of all persons in a particular class, i.e., all Blacks are this; all Jews are that; all Italians are something else. At the same time I reserve my right to dislike or oppose any human being of any kind on an individual basis for cause.

I deplore the disgraceful manner in which Blacks were willfully and deliberately abused in this country for decades. I'll never forget my first sally into the deep South in the summer of 1951.

While attending Holy Cross, I joined an officer training program offered by the United States Marine Corps which required me to spend that summer at Parris Island, the Marine Corps Recruit Depot in Beaufort, South Carolina. I boarded the train for Parris Island at the old Pennsylvania Station totally oblivious to the shock that was in store for me. All the railroad stations in the South had separate bathrooms and waiting rooms for Blacks, and other facilities for "Whites Only." Vendors treated Blacks with disdain while others simply refused to deal with them at all.

On the weekends we were permitted to leave Parris Island. We would go to either Savannah, Georgia, or Charlestown, North Carolina. There we found that Blacks were not allowed in White hotels or restaurants, and they had to sit in the back of the bus when they used that form of transportation. Nor were they allowed in the "White" schools or the "White" sections of public parks. All of the jobs they held were menial, and they were universally and publicly referred to as "niggers." All of this flew in the face of everything I had been taught since childhood, and I was horrified. While things have improved vastly since those terrible days, I think that we still have a continuing obligation to see to it that Blacks are afforded equal opportunities in all respects.

Having said that, I have reservations with respect to establishing quotas in favor of Blacks. Why? First, I think that "set-asides" discriminate against others. Second, I don't like the basic fundamental assumption involved in such "set-asides" namely that Blacks can't compete with others "head to head." It's demeaning and I don't believe it's true. Third, I'll bet that many Blacks agree with me as to my second reservation above.

My grandfather taught me as a boy to treat all persons with dignity and respect and I've tried to do so ever since. But I think "political correctness" is forced, artificial and disingenuous.

Although I am registered Democrat, I have voted for Republicans, Conservatives and Liberals.

But on the basis of the foregoing, what am I? Am I a liberal, a conservative, a socialist, or none of the above. Those on the far left would probably classify me as an "arch conservative" while those on the far right would probably classify me as a "knee-jerk liberal." "None of the above" is the correct answer and that's the case with most reasonable people. You can't put reasonable people in a "political box" because they don't belong in one and don't want to be there.

Political boxes are for non-thinking automatons; the "frothing at the mouth" fanatics and political "haters" at both ends of the political spectrum. They put everyone else in a box and want to be perceived as being in one of those boxes themselves because they desperately want to be regarded as "intelligent," "caring," "tough" or "super patriots" and they are of the pathetic belief that that's how you get there!

They associate almost exclusively with each other and are highly intolerant of those who disagree with them. They don't discuss contrary views but rather dismiss them. They are totally predictable and boring.

My friend, Ed Koch, puts it another way and very briefly when he says "If you agree with me on 8 out of 12 issues, that's normal and understandable. If you agree with me on all 12 issues, see a psychiatrist." He puts it even more succinctly when he describes himself as "a liberal with sanity."

I have always been interested in public service and have engaged in it in a variety of ways and to a substantial degree.

Frank Hogan served as District Attorney of New York County for 32 years and was an avid proponent of public service. I served under him as an Assistant District Attorney for 5½ years. In my judgment, he was the finest public servant that ever held public office.

This is a picture of Frank Hogan and the members of the Supreme Court Bureau, the Bureau that tried felony cases and the one in which I served. Hogan is in the middle of the front row and I am on his left. There are many others in the picture who went on to brilliant careers in the public sector. They are: Bronx District Attorney Burt Roberts, Supreme Court Judge Larry Burnstein, Federal District Court Judge John F. Keenan, Criminal Court Judge Irving Lang, Criminal Court Judge Jim Yeargin, Appellate Division Court Judge Leonard Sandler, Criminal Court Judge Ed Davidowitz, and Criminal Court Judge Mel Glass. See if you can find them in the picture! This gives you an idea of the caliber of persons Hogan chose to serve on his staff.

Hogan would say: "Public service is the highest calling to which a person can aspire, save the cloth" (the "cloth" meaning the religious service). By his lights, the betrayal of a public trust was the most egregious crime in the Penal Code, and God help those who did, no matter who they were!

He was keenly ware of the enormous power that persons in public service wield and felt deeply about their solemn duty and obligation to wield it with great care, fairness and, of course, with uncompromising and unflinching integrity. A Governor, a Mayor, a Senator, a Congressman, a Judge, a county executive, a state legislator influences society more with a sweep of a pen than most people in the private sector impact society in a lifetime. And so, it's an area that should be served by the best.

I'm reminded of an incident involving Frank Hogan and me that I think you will find amusing.

In 1973, William Vanden Heuvel, a former Bobby Kennedy aide, ran in a Democratic primary election against Frank Hogan for the Democratic nomination for District Attorney of New York County.

By that time I had been out of the office for eight years and Hogan asked me to get involved in his campaign which, of course, I did in a very substantial way. I galvanized all former Hogan Assistant DA's, raised money and prevailed upon my cousin Tom Shanahan, Jr. to serve as campaign treasurer. Hogan won with 80% of the vote!

Hogan first became District Attorney of New York County in January 1942. Everyone who ever worked for him called him "Mr. Hogan." The only person who did not was his Chief Assistant DA, Al Scotti, who called him "Boss." No one ever referred to him as "Frank."

On the night of his victory over Vanden Heuvel, I was with Hogan when Vanden Heuvel called to concede the election. Hogan was sitting behind a desk and I was sitting in front of it. Hogan was very gracious to Vanden Heuvel; congratulated him in running a decent campaign and encouraged him to pursue a career in public service.

While that was going on, I decided that when Hogan hung up the phone, I would get up, extend my hand and say "Congratulations Frank! And I did all of that except instead of "Congratulations Frank" I said: "Congratulations Frrr — Mr. Hogan." I just couldn't do it!

One of the problems of today is that there is a dreadful paucity in the public sector of able and competent people who act from conscience and do what's right regardless of political consequences. Fiorello LaGuardia and Ed Koch are examples of public servants who acted in the best interests of the common good, without regard to adverse political fall out.

And as I've suggested, Mayor Michael Bloomberg is another example of a public official who by and large acts from conscience and does what he thinks is right without regard to adverse political fall out. For example, he banned smoking at a time when there was overwhelming opposition to such a ban and precious little demand for it! And now he's acclaimed for having done so. In addition, he raised taxes when he first came into office, because he thought it was necessary. More recently he took the position that Muslims had the absolute right to build a mosque in close proximity to ground zero no matter what and he's never backed off that position, although others have.

The vast majority recognize the basic religious right involved under the First Amendment but contend that such right should not be exercised for other reasons; that it's not the right thing to do, given the attendant circumstances. I agree with the majority but admire and respect Bloomberg for adhering to what he believes is right despite the fact that it is extremely unpopular. The fact that he is acting from conscience is by far the most important aspect; the fact that I disagree with him is a secondary consideration.

But at the present time, the vast majority of politicians are motivated solely by an all consuming desire to get themselves or someone else elected or re-elected. As a result, political polls reign supreme and dictate political conduct rather than conscience.

Our two major political parties have become polarized for political purposes. The mutual respect and goodwill that existed between the political adversaries such as Senator Al D'Amato and Senator Pat Moynihan which often resulted in compromises in the best interests of the common good has evaporated and Americans are damn mad.

Just take a look at the recent gubernatorial election in New York during which Carl Paladino received a surprising number of votes in an election that should have been an across the board avalanche! Why? The voters in New York are so angry they can't see straight!

Today's politics has become a dirty and vicious business like never before where "anything goes." Charges, allegations, assertions, insinuations, innuendos, obsession with the fixation of blame, willful and deliberate misinterpretations, half truths, wholesale lying, faking, ducking, dodging, acting, hiding, false denials, misleading advertising, threats, intimidation, false promises, posturing, pandering, taking or claiming credit for something done by someone else, digging up dirt and defining words in a misleading manner, and blaming predecessors for current problems.

Most infuriating, is the notion that all of that is "OK" because it's "politics!" What a sad and pathetic commentary! Because of the importance of the matters in which they are engaged, politicians should be held to even higher ethical standards than others rather than lower standards! And should they ever pull themselves out of the doldrums and attain such ethical standards, they ought to be paid more than those in the private sector because of the comparative importance of the work they perform!

Wrongdoing and highly inappropriate conduct on the part of public servants at the highest levels, born of unbelievable arrogance, has become commonplace and often goes unpunished.

What is going to emerge from all of this political chaos? I think that going forward, party affiliation and political labels such as "liberal" and "conservative" will count for less and less. Voters will be seeking out candidates that are non-partisan and apolitical. They will be looking for persons who will act on the basis of what they believe is the right thing to do – whatever that may be, as long as it's not simply for purposes of political advancement. They will be looking for people who are intelligent, informed and deeply devoted and dedicated to doing what's right no matter what the political consequences.

A new day is dawning.

The plus side of public service is the satisfaction one derives from doing it honestly and well. For example, I served as a "hands on" Chairman of Battery Park City "pro bono" for 14 years, from 1996 to 2010.

This is Mayor Bloomberg, Rose, James and I at Gracie Mansion

During that period we transformed Battery Park City from a "stop-over" to a fully developed residential community, preserved it as one of the world's most important financial centers and introduced acclaimed cultural features such as the Holocaust Museum and the Irish Hunger Memorial. Moreover, we led the nation in the building of "green" buildings. For all practical purposes we completed the "build out" of Battery Park City.

The pride and satisfaction that I derive from those accomplishments cannot be measured. I know that one day my grandchildren will walk through Battery Park City and say to those with them "Look at what my Grandpa did!" It doesn't get any better than that and you can't buy it. That's the kind of reward that one can derive from public service!

Some people think that I wield great power. Recently, the *Irish America* magazine included me among "The Legal 100" — Irish Lawyers and Judges Across the United States who "Share a Passion for the Law and Pride in their Heritage." A short time ago, Long Island Catholic described me as "one of the most influential attorneys in the U.S." In 1998, the *New York Times* published a feature article on me entitled: "Power Broker with Blarney in His Pen."

I've been around a long time and involved in a significant number of high-profile projects. As a result, I have a lot of friends and know many people in high places.

Let me assure you, however, that I don't have nearly the clout that many attribute to me. Nonetheless, I've always made it a point to let people think whatever they want. Nor do I correct them when they suggest that I have more power than I do! And so the myth goes on and I have become more and more powerful without doing a thing! It's all in the eye of the beholder and that's "OK" with me!

When you exert influence, it is wise to do it quietly and without fanfare. Staying below the radar screen will make you more effective in the long run.

It is essential to insure that you never embarrass the person from whom you are seeking assistance. If you do, it may be the last assistance you'll ever receive from anyone.

I will not get involved in any cause unless (1) it is the right thing to do; (2) it can be accomplished with relative ease; and (3) it will not in any way embarrass the person from whom I am seeking assistance.

When asked to intervene on behalf of someone I will frequently ask: "I know how this will help you, but how will it help the person from whom you are seeking assistance?" With that kind of an approach you will acquire a reputation for honesty and integrity and enjoy trust and confidence.

Chapter 13: *God, the Church and Related Matters*

THE EXISTENCE OF GOD

I believe in God as do most people. Atheists in this country represent 8% of our population

From the beginning of mankind, people have posited belief in and worshipped deities. For many, the deity was the sun as was the case when St. Patrick converted the people of Ireland. To help him convert those sun worshippers, Patrick imposed the sun on the cross and thus the Celtic cross came into existence. (Incidentally, the added physical strength the sun afforded, allowed Celtic crosses to endure far longer than standard crosses). Many others worshipped fire. That innate urge to worship some form of deity from the beginning of mankind speaks to the existence of a deity of some sort.

But arguments for the existence of God are many and compelling. They have been studied by scholars for centuries.

At Holy Cross College, the Jesuits (Members of the Society of Jesus, all of whom add the Letters "SJ" after their names) introduced me to the argument of the "uncaused cause." It made sense to me then and it still does.

As we go through life we become aware of the reality that for every effect there is a cause. Think if you will, of something indeed anything in our world which is without a cause.

Interestingly, science, often regarded as the nemesis of theism, constantly and unfailingly discovers and verifies the causes of effects. Studies for causes sometimes take extended periods of time but eventually succeed! And we never stop the search for a cause because we know that there must be one.

We witness causality and breathtaking intelligence in nature, phenomena, designs, living creatures and things every day — the rising and setting of the sun, the seasons, weather, the planetary system, the actions of the oceans, the workings of the moon, the workings, development and interactions of man, animals, birds, fishes, insects, flowers, trees and on and on.

How did it all happen? Where did it all come from? Is it conceivable that it all came from nothing? Is it possible that no one set all of this in motion? Such a conclusion flies in the face of all human experience.

The only logical cause is an uncaused cause – a deity and an intelligent deity. We know from everyday life that the product can never be greater than the creator.

Speaking of the Society of Jesus (S.J.), I have a story to tell.

The Jesuits and the Benedictines had a dispute over a very esoteric theological point. Eventually, the question went to the heads of both orders but could not be resolved. The question was then submitted to the Vatican but again without resolution. Finally, the question was sent to the Pope, whom after considerable thought and many hours of prayer, advised the heads of the orders that he was submitting the question to God.

Shortly thereafter, he summoned them to the Vatican to hear the reading of a telegram from God. The telegram read as follows:

"The Benedictines are right.

Signed,

God, S.J."

That's an old Jesuitical joke! That's the way they are, you know.

Back to the existence of God and some thoughts about an afterlife. Adolph Hitler was probably the greatest monster the world has ever produced. I would be enormously dismayed if he were not punished in an afterlife for his atrocities and all of the pain and suffering he willfully and deliberately visited on millions and millions of people.

Conversely, Mother Theresa lived her life in abject poverty and devoted herself totally, wholly and completely to serving the poor. I would be terribly distressed if she were not rewarded in an afterlife. Justice, which is an integral spiritual part of our innate being, cries out for that kind of punishment and reward. Where did our innate human thirst for justice come from? Did it come from nowhere? Did it come into existence out of nothing? Such concepts are intellectually absurd.

A somewhat related but yet different argument for the existence of God is the existence of the natural moral law. All reasonable persons have recognized that certain conduct is wrong. For example, all reasonable persons would agree that the unjust taking of another's life is wrong; that stealing and lying without just cause are wrong. And there is a universally accepted list of good works as well. Who wrote that universal code of conduct? Where did it come from? Is it conceivable that it had no source; that it came out of nothing? Again and again we come back to an uncaused cause infinitely superior to all effects.

RELIGIONS

Before leaving the discussion about the existence of God, I want to comment on the authenticity of the Gospels, which of course, deal with the life of Jesus Christ.

I am satisfied that the authenticity of the Gospels has been established as has the authenticity of many of the works on George Washington, Abraham Lincoln and myriad others. Such studies relating to the Gospel have been conducted again and again by the great scholars of the world. And so I accept unreservedly the concept that Jesus Christ was the Son of God.

Obviously, I am aware that many disagree — Muslims, Jews, Buddhists, and a host of others. I respect those differing ideas and the right of those who believe in them to worship accordingly. And while I am a

Catholic, I respect the teachings of the many Protestant sects which differ from Catholic beliefs.

The followers of all of the religions of the world have every right to espouse their own beliefs. But it is of great importance that we all come together with respect and support, for the right of others to disagree. Far too many wars have been and continue to be religiously based.

When I started practicing law at Robinson Silverman & Pearce, Ben Robinson, the senior partner of our firm and a very wise man, required all of us to have a sign on our desks which read, "You can disagree without being disagreeable."

Which brings to mind a true story about the late Cardinal Cushing of Boston who was a close friend and spiritual adviser of the Kennedy clan.

At the time of the terrible fire at Filene's Basement many years ago, Cardinal Cushing was a young priest and responded to the fire. Upon arrival he saw an elderly man on the ground who was apparently in extremis.

Cushing knelt next to the man to administer the Last Rites. He leaned over the man and whispered in his ear, "Do you believe in God the Father, God the Son and God the Holy Ghost?" Whereupon the man opened one eye and responded: "I'm dying — and you want me to answer a riddle!"

ATHEISTS

The first part of the First Amendment to the United States Constitution reads as follows: "Congress shall make no law respecting an establishment of religion, or prohibiting the free exercise thereof . . ." It then goes on to protect other rights such as freedom of speech. The second part is separate and distinct from the first.

America has always been and remains a theistic country. Our first settlers came to this country from England to escape a state religion that prohibited them from practicing the religions of their choice. That was the reason why the First Amendment was adopted as it relates to religion. That part of the First Amendment prohibits one religion from being treated more favorably as against any other religion.

It was never intended to protect atheism which by definition is god-lessness. The essence of all religions is the serving of a God – be it God the Father, Jesus Christ, the Son of God, the Holy Spirit, the Holy Trinity, Allah, Buddha, Yahweh or Vishnu. The early history of our country and all of the documents that established it abound in references to God as do our public buildings and our currency. Nowhere is there any reference to protecting atheism.

And yet, some Supreme Court Justices have suggested that atheism, which espouses godlessness and therefore rejects all religions, is protected by that part of the First Amendment which was intended to protect all religions! It's startling.

I don't have a problem with persons who espouse atheism, deny the existence of God and debunk religions. That's protected under the speech portion of the First Amendment. But to suggest that atheism is a religion, when by definition it is the absence thereof, is absurd. Moreover there are some atheists who from time to time seek to do away with the religious rights of the vast majority of Americans who believe in a god. That is completely unacceptable. To put it another way, it was never intended that atheism be our state "religion."

THE CHURCH

I am a true believer in the Catholic Church and a practicing Catholic in the sense that I attend mass on Sundays and holidays and defend the Faith.

But, I am lacking woefully in the manner in which I conduct my daily life. I am indeed a sinner. I don't say that for the purpose of conveying the impression that I am humble. I am not that either, as many of my close friends will readily attest! Nonetheless, I'm a true believer.

One of the great joys of my life was when I met Pope John Paul II at the residence of Cardinal O'Connor when he visited New York City in 1995.

Although a true believer, I think that there are aspects of Church instruction which warrant discussion. I believe that over the years, the Church has been overly fixated on sex.

God created men and women. That's basic and fundamental Catholic doctrine. In doing so. He saw fit to instill in them sexual desire. As we know from experience that desire is probably the strongest instinct in human nature except the instinct for survival. The purpose of the installation of that desire was obviously the perpetuation of the human race. How has the Church dealt with that God-implanted desire?

Catholics and particularly young Catholics are told that sexual intercourse is prohibited until marriage which is obviously understandable and perfectly appropriate. In addition, they are often told that they must not "entertain" impure thoughts; that they must avoid the "occasions" of sin; that all solitary sins are "serious" in nature; that "lusting" after a person is sinful conduct; that they must not read books or look at movies or videos that deal with sex and on and on, despite incessant and powerful sexual desires.

The result is that many Catholics are often engaged in moral struggles of enormous proportions. When does concupiscence become sinful conduct? Have I crossed the line? If so, was it my fault?

They are frequently beset with an unwarranted sense of guilt which sometimes distracts them from and dilutes their sensitivity as to other moral principles which are at least of equal significance such as refraining from deliberately hurting and inflicting pain on another human being by act or words.

I'm not advocating the elimination of all sexual restraints but rather a re-examination of the subject matter; the degree of emphasis placed upon it and insuring that other principles are not neglected or reduced in importance.

Having said all of that, I'm reminded of something Cardinal O'Connor once said: "Practicing the Catholic Faith is not like attending a smorgasbord at which you take what you want and leave the rest behind!" He never flinched!

ABORTION

I oppose abortion. I believe that a fetus is a human being from the first moment of conception. If allowed to run its natural course, most assuredly and undeniably a child will emerge — not a kitten, a bird or a bunny, but a human being.

While I can somewhat understand disagreement as to the first moment of conception, what I don't understand for the life of me, are those who oppose a ban on partial birth abortion. As the name suggests, partial birth abortion has to do with the destruction of a fully developed child partially out of the womb!

I think that those who are pro-choice make a very serious mistake in opposing the ban on partial birth abortion because they put themselves in the position of having to deal with the absurd proposition that the difference between a blob of ganglia and a precious human being is the act of complete passage of the child through the womb, as opposed to a child who has partially passed through the womb! Put another way, the child who is partially through the womb may be destroyed, but the instant it is completely through the womb it is fully protected by our laws! These basic and fundamental observations may not be ignored or simply brushed aside but rather cry out for answers. Unfortunately for those who oppose a ban on partial birth abortion, there are none!

To carry it a step further — if it's "OK" to destroy a fully developed child which is partially out of the womb why can't you destroy it the moment it is completely out of the womb? And if you can do it then, why not a minute, an hour, a day or a week after birth, particularly if it is defective? Is society ready for that? I don't think so! Shame on the politicians who oppose the ban on partial birth abortion for political reasons. It's infanticide!

ANNULMENTS AND DIVORCES

While the Church has largely eradicated the notion that wealthy and powerful Catholics are able to obtain marital annulments not available to others, vestiges linger on that must be completely stamped out.

I also think that banning divorced persons from receiving communion in certain cases is sometimes too harsh and counterproductive. Each such case should be examined closely on an individual basis.

CHILD ABUSE

But of course the Church's most serious problem today has to do with sexual abuse of children by Catholic clergymen.

There is no question that such horrendous abuses took place and that certain members of the Church's hierarchy failed to deal with them in an appropriate manner. During that period, the Church was of the mistaken belief that a pedophile could be cured and many in the psychiatric community agreed that such was the case. Justice, forgiveness and redemption came into play. Ill-conceived notions about "scandal" within the Church were in vogue. As a result of all of that, grave injuries were inflicted.

But with the revelation that a pedophile cannot be cured, changes began to set in and finally took hold. The Church for almost a decade now has acknowledged and made amends for such wrong-doing and exposed and punished such wrong-doers. Measures have been taken to insure that such atrocities do not occur going forward.

Yet problems continue. Cases which took place decades ago, during that earlier period when the Church labored under the mistaken belief that pedophilia was curable, crop up from time to time and wrongfully suggest that the Church has failed to take corrective action. Such cases will continue to crop up and there will always be valid concerns about false claims which undeniably exist. Moreover, there are some who seize upon this issue in order to disparage the Church and its teachings.

But before moving on to the next chapter, I have another ramble (rarely used as a noun).

MOTHER THERESA AND THE EMPIRE STATE BUILDING

On August 26, 2010, the United States Postal Service honored the 100th anniversary of the birth of Mother Theresa. During her life,

Mother Theresa received 124 awards, including the Nobel Peace Prize, the Presidential Medal of Freedom and the Congressional Medal of Freedom.

A request was made of the Empire State Building that its tower lights feature blue and white, the colors of Mother Theresa's Order, on August 26, 2010, the same day upon which the U.S. Postal Service honored the 100th anniversary of her birth.

The Building denied that request without explanation! Obviously those who control the building saw fit to protect us all from the grave and irreparable harm that would be visited upon all of us if such a request were granted!

But what I find particularly ironic is the following:

Our former four-time Governor, Al Smith, ran for the presidency of the United States in 1928. History demonstrates unequivocally that his defeat was attributable to anti-Catholicism. After his defeat, he built the Empire State Building! He must be rolling in his grave! The great Empire State Building deserves better and those responsible for that idiotic decision should be ousted!

The horrors of war are mind boggling. I've never experienced them. But I've lived through World War II, the Korean War, the Vietnamese War, the Gulf War, the Iraqi War and now the Afghanistan War, and I've read a great deal of military history.

Many of those histories are devoted in large measure to extolling the virtues of military commanders involved. That kind of treatment sometimes takes away from the excruciating pain, long suffering and misery that is the essence of war. Military histories frequently overlook the many blunders so common to all warfare because of its nature and sometimes even horrendous decisions motivated by the personal ambitions of military persons in command are ignored or glossed over.

Recent military histories are more realistic as to the nature of war and more forthcoming with respect to disastrous decisions motivated by the personal egos of military leaders. The further you get from the battle time wise, the more truth comes to the fore.

I have in mind military histories such as *Army at Dawn*, for which author Rick Atkinson won the Pulitzer Prize, *The Day of Battle*, also by Atkinson, *Anzio* by Lloyd Clark, *The Battle*, a new history of the battle of Waterloo by Allessandro Barbero, and *The Coldest Winter* by David Haberstrom.

Incidentally, good military histories have intelligible maps which allow you to follow the battles as they are described in the book! Military histories without such maps limp.

But before leaving the subject of war and all its horrors, allow me to quote the former Commandant of the United States Marine Corp., General James T. Conway:

"No one wants war but someone has got to know how to do it!"

Anyone who thinks we are not at war with Muslim terrorists is a fool or hopelessly misguided. And any elected politician who refuses to accept it ought to be thrown out of office.

The killing of human beings because they are not members of a particular religious sect is mind-boggling and may not be countenanced under any set of circumstances least of all, on the basis of religion!

Nor is there any justification for those who engage in such terrorists killings to be tried in a civil court. Who are we trying to impress and why? What is the principle involved? If it is being done as a matter of principle, why are some being tried in civil courts and others before military tribunals? If principle is involved why shouldn't it be applied to all?

And if such persons are to be tried in civil court they should receive all of the protections that a civil court provides, not just some. Otherwise the whole procedure is a farce. Which raises a question as to statements made by Attorney General Eric Holder at the very time he announced that five Muslim terrorists would be tried in the civil court.

On that occasion he said that he was "quite confident" that the Justice Department could produce enough evidence to get convictions and that "ultimately they must face the ultimate justice" — the death penalty. That is a gross and wanton violation of the rights of any person tried in a civil court!

Another thought — the five Muslim terrorists to be tried civilly may well make a motion to dismiss the charges against them for lack of a speedy trial! Some have been in custody at Guantanamo for very substantial periods of time. Can you imagine?

In London, newspapers don't purport to be "fair," "balanced," "non-partisan" or "non-political" in reporting the news. They are openly and notoriously "liberal," "conservative," or whatever, and their news reporting reflects those beliefs. They make no pretenses. They have agendas and they give vent to them with joy and exuberance. How refreshing!

Sad to say, in the main, we don't have that kind of journalistic honesty and integrity in the United States. Our newspapers sanctimoniously purport to be above the fray in presenting the news and solemnly proclaim that they simply report unadorned facts without trying to promote or denigrate officials, candidates or causes. There is no slanting of the news they say; no effort to influence readers one way or the other; no hidden agenda; it's all on the level! What hypocrisy! And everyone knows it.

There was a time when the printed word was held sacred and presumed valid; a time when ethical standards were rigidly applied by journalists in presenting the news. Some journalists and newspapers still apply those standards, but they are hard to find!

Before proceeding further, I hasten to say that the journalistic hypocrisy to which I refer is by no means the exclusive property of the left or the right, the Democrats, Republicans, or any other groups. It's across the board.

The newspaper industry is being replaced by the electronic media and computers. Getting the news in these ways is easier, faster, cheaper, sometimes more complete and frequently more enjoyable. And so, newspaper circulation is falling off dramatically and newspapers are going out of business day after day.

What you read in newspapers is usually a day old and an ever dwindling number of people have any interest in editorials. By and large, newspapers are losing their political clout. As a matter of fact, younger people no longer read newspapers at all. The trouble is that the electronic media is just as bad, if not worse, in the manner in which they present the news.

Wouldn't it be a great joy if a newspaper or a news program on television came along which really and truly just presented unadulterated facts and left the conclusions to be drawn to the audience! People are perfectly capable of making up their own minds. I think that America is thirsting for such a journalistic development, and a new day is dawning.

ADVERTISING

I'm aware that in the world of advertising, the name of the game is to get attention, no matter what! And so, we have television ads such as the one in which the world's most consummate "smart ass" asks stupid questions in an effort to promote Geico insurance. I can't stand him and I would love to smack him across the face! Yes, he gets attention, but the question is: does he sell the product in view of the fact that he is so incredibly obnoxious? I don't think so.

Similarly, the dumbest ad on television is Capital One Bank's ad featuring a host of cavorting cavemen. Do people really want to put their hard earned savings into the hands of a band of silly cavemen? No way.

What are the best ads on television? In my opinion, they are the Geico lizard and the Aflac duck – going away!

A great deal of advertising in the media is ridiculous, particularly as it relates to certain medical products. Such advertisements frequently go something like this: "This product is not for everyone – and we urge you to consult your physician before using it. Its side effects include dizziness, temporary loss of vision and/or hearing, severe headaches, nausea, violent vomiting, deep depression, suicidal tendencies, cancer, heart disease, palsy, gangrene and herpes" (a slight exaggeration).

It seems to me that many would be frightened off by products laden with such dire caveats – even if it were penicillin. Moreover, any product that carries with it multiple serious side effects shouldn't be on the market in the first place.

The lawyers who write these warnings want to be absolutely certain that they have fully protected their clients against any and all possible legal contingencies, however remote, and more importantly, protected themselves. The fact that their clients may realize precious little revenue as a result never occurs to them or if it does, they don't care, as long as they are protected.

Then, of course, we have products like Viagra. Invariably, they conclude with a stern admonition to see a doctor immediately if an erection lasts for a week or more (another slight exaggeration). Note that they never tell you what they expect the doctor to do – or suggest what you are supposed to do in the meantime! The nonsense the advertising world gets away with in the media every day is mind boggling and it costs a fortune! You don't suppose that Viagra admonition is really intended to promote the product — do you?

TV ENTERTAINMENT

Newton N. Minow was appointed Chairman of the Federal Communications Commission by President John F. Kennedy. At a convention of the National Association of Broadcasters on May 9, 1961, he described television programming as a "vast wasteland" and indeed it was. The problem is that aside from more and better programming in the public interest, it has gotten worse.

In years gone by, television presented Jackie Gleason and the *Honeymooners*, Sid Caesar, and the *Show of Shows*, the Ed Sullivan Show, the Jack Benny Show, George Burns and Gracie Allen, Bob Hope Specials, Groucho Marx and *You Bet Your Life*, Lucille Ball and *I Love Lucy*, *Mash*, *Alfred Hitchcock Presents*, and the *Twilight Zone*. Millions of people looked forward to and watched those shows every week without fail. And now they're all gone and nothing has replaced them except sex, violence, crime, corruption, pathetic attempts at comedy and canned laughter! It's sad!

All I watch on television are the news, sports, old movies, public interest programs and historical specials. And I am not alone!

So how should one spend leisure time? My recommendation — reading. My favorite pastime is reading American history, public speeches, the classics, biographies of all types and books about power and politics. I particularly enjoy military history because the cauldron of a battle involving life and death often brings out the best and the worst in people.

I read in bed, in my den in front of the fireplace, in my backyard, at the beach, on a train and on an airplane.

I love to discuss and exchange books with other avid readers and do so with my dear friend, John Zuccotti, regularly.

Lately, I've been doing the same with my grandson, James, who is a voracious reader at age 11! We've just gotten into Sherlock Holmes.

A new day is dawning.

Chapter 16: *The Making of a Great Lawyer*

On March 7, 2006, I addressed law students from six law schools in the New York area at Fordham Law School. The subject was "The Making of the Great Lawyer."

My remarks were printed in the New York Law Journal, and reprinted in the U.S. and overseas. This is what I said:

When John Feerick asked me to speak tonight, he suggested that I share with you some of my thoughts on the ingredients that go into the making of the "great" lawyer. Accordingly that is my topic and in the process I'll pass on some unsolicited advice.

I was trained by the Jesuits and they taught me the crucial importance of defining terms something that is woefully lacking, indeed almost non-existent not only in the law but in the parlance of the day.

The great lawyers define terms and usually at the beginning of a discussion or an argument. A failure to do so can properly subject one to the charge: "You don't know what you're talking about."

Having said that, I better tell you what I mean by "great." In the context of this discussion, "great" brings to mind myriad words and phrases like: "decent," "honorable," "noble," "conscientious," "caring," "hard-working," "dedicated," "devoted," "able," "competent," "learned," "superior in quality," and "uncompromising integrity." Greatness in a lawyer is all of that but we must go beyond a mere recitation of words and phrases to fully appreciate its meaning.

In order to measure "greatness" in a lawyer, it is important to remember that the primary purpose of the law is the doing of justice. It's not "getting people off;" winning high-profile cases or making money but rather the implementation of moral rightness. We are entrusted with that grave responsibility. And so the great lawyers have a thirst for justice, rail against injustice and fight to right a wrong. I'm reminded of the motto on the coat of arms of my friend, the late John Cardinal

O'Connor: "There can be no love without justice."

Great lawyers recognize their duty to contribute to the common good and improve the society in which we live and great lawyers teach and encourage fledgling lawyers to do the same.

Great lawyers are keenly aware of the fact that the rule of law is the difference between an ordered society and the law of the Jungle wherein the powerful devour the weak. And so the great lawyers respect, protect and preserve the body of law, improve it and enforce it.

Unfortunately, the practice of law which ought to be an honorable profession, to an alarming extent, has become just another business. More and more, discussions among lawyers deal with subjects like: billable hours, percentage of realization, merchandizing, generating more business, increasing fees, recouping expenses, hiring lawyers that will contribute to the "bottom line," collecting fees, merging with other firms to get a larger share of the market and advertising in the media, most of which is disgraceful.

I'm fully aware of the necessity of making a living and supporting a family. Indeed family always comes first. But making money should never become the be-all and end-all of practicing law.

There was a time when firms encouraged associates and partners to perform pro bono work and rewarded it financially. Many firms still do and I applaud them. But many ban it, discourage it, or pay it lip service because it reduces revenue for firms. Some firms do not provide remuneration for those who perform it — a sad commentary.

I digress at this point to congratulate the law students in the audience from six law schools, who are already engaged in pro bono work. I not only urge you to continue that work but exhort you to consider entering public service when you graduate. Public servants exert infinitely more influence in improving our society than lawyers in the private sector.

Moreover, I want to salute my alma mater, Fordham Law School, for all it has done to promote public service for 100 years. No law school in this country has done more!

The great lawyer need not be a legal encyclopedia but is grounded in basic and fundamental legal principles; thinks like a lawyer and has the capacity to find the applicable law in any given case. Obviously there is no excuse or explanation for not knowing the law or misinterpreting it when it is clear. Many a client has paid a severe price for such a failure.

In the 1960's when I was an assistant district attorney in the office of the late great Frank Hogan, the District Attorney of N.Y. County, there was a highly popular program on television known as "The $64,000 Question." Contestants, many of whom were celebrities, would sweat and stew in a small cubicle with daunting music playing in the background, in an effort to answer a series of questions that would result in winning the grand prize of $64,000. It turned out that many of the contestants received the questions and answers in advance. In the main, the program was a colossal fraud on the public and Hogan was called upon to investigate the matter to ascertain whether criminal conduct was involved.

Because the program was presented to the public as "entertainment," there was no crime. Accordingly those contestants who testified before the Grand Jury and admitted that they got the questions and answers before the show, were not charged with any crime and their admissions remain secret to this day because of the secrecy which attaches to Grand Jury testimony.

On the other hand, those contestants who lied to the Grand Jury, by claiming that they did not get the questions and answers in advance, were convicted of perjury, and their careers were ruined. That would not have happened if they had simply told the truth! Obviously some lawyers did their legal home work and others did not with a catastrophic result!

The great lawyer is not only fully aware of every legal aspect of a case but pursues the facts with relentless and unyielding determination.

The late Mel Glass served as an Assistant DA in New York County at the same time I did and we were friends.

On August 18, 1963 Emily Hoffert and Janice Wylie were brutally murdered in an apartment they shared at 57 East 88th Street in Manhattan. They were very attractive young career women, well on their way to the top in their respective fields. Emily was the daughter of a Chicago doctor and Janice was the niece of the noted author Philip Wylie.

The particulars of the killings were gruesome. Both died of multiple stab wounds and Emily's head was almost severed from her body. I saw the photographs from the murder scene and almost became ill. The case received national media attention and the Police Department was under pressure to find the killer.

One of the peculiar aspects of the case was that following the murders, the murderer took a shower; washed the knives used in the murders; placed them side-by-side on a radiator and attempted to straighten out the apartment!

Mel Glass, although not assigned to the homicide bureau, got involved in the case, in clear violation of a strict office protocol. At the outset he ascertained from his sister Blanche, a psychiatrist, that the killer was beset with a sick and all-compelling obsession with cleanliness.

The police arrested George Whitmore, a young black man from Brooklyn for the murders and procured a written confession that was replete with minute details about the killings and the inside of the apartment. Because of those extensive and intimate details everyone concluded that Whitmore had to be the killer everyone that is except Mel Glass who pointed out that the police had knowledge of those details as well as the killer.

Glass inquired about and learned that Whitmore was dirty and disheveled at the time of the arrest which didn't square with what Blanche had told him. Moreover, it was highly unusual for a young black man from Brooklyn, to be operating in such a neighborhood. Time does not allow me to provide you with all of the details but the end result of Glass's unauthorized investigation was astonishing.

Glass caught, tried and convicted Richard Robles, the real killer. George Whitmore was exonerated. Police officers were disciplined and Glass' dogged pursuit of the facts in the case, in the face of unbelievable obstacles, gave rise to a television series called *Kojak*, starring Telly Savalas. What Mel Glass did in that case is the stuff of which greatness is made!

There are other features of practicing law which in my opinion go to "greatness" although others may disagree.

I believe that the great lawyer does not restrict himself or herself to a single area of law as so many lawyers do but rather embraces and plunges into new areas with relish. Diversity expands your knowledge and increases your value as a lawyer. Besides, it's interesting and fun. While there is a need for specialists in certain areas, there is far too much unnecessary specialization in the law.

Moreover, I envision the great lawyer as a generalist in another sense; a lawyer who tries cases, negotiates and drafts agreements, settles disputes, prepares briefs, argues appeals and contributes to the common good. In short, I see the great lawyer as the "complete" lawyer. And I see the "complete" lawyer as the better lawyer because the parts and pieces that make up the practice of law are interrelated. For example, I believe that a lawyer who has tried cases involving language interpretation is better able to draft legal documents because he or she is better suited to anticipate challenges.

And for me, the great lawyer is always civil, never indulges in pejorative language and is always magnanimous in victory!

But while some may differ as to whether some of the elements I've discussed go to greatness, there can be no dispute about the fact that the great lawyer is a person of unflinching and undiluted integrity who protects his or her good name with a vengeance. I am appalled by some lawyers who believe that their job is to provide a client with a winning story. Truth telling is the fabric of an ordered society that must be upheld at all costs, especially in the law.

Another indisputable hallmark of the great lawyer is the ability to exercise sound judgment and discretion. "Here's my situation — what should I do?" asks the client. That's frequently where the great lawyers are separated from others. Sometimes it's easy, sometimes it's hard. But it takes time and experience, knowledge and savvy, an understanding of human nature, God given talent and luck to prevail regularly in that all important area.

Sometimes the answer is: "Do nothing," "Settle" or "Mediate." That won't generate legal fees and it may not be what a client wants to hear but if it's the right course to follow that's the advise the great lawyer renders.

And of course there are other elements that go into the mix of the great lawyer:

- The art of being able to speak and write grammatically, clearly and succinctly. Unfortunately many young lawyers are lacking in these areas.

- The ability to pursue a line of questioning to the end. The great lawyer is never put off by glib responses, stock expressions, attempted diversions, counter-attacks or lies.

- The willingness to work hard and to place a client's interests and needs above ones own, without sacrificing personal integrity or neglecting family.

And I am sure there are others. While the ability to employ humor in timely fashion may not be a prerequisite for greatness, it certainly can help.

At this point some of you are probably saying, "Given all those criteria, it's virtually impossible for anyone to become a great lawyer!" While there is merit in that contention, allow me the following observations:

Notoriety and fame, stature and money are not prerequisites for greatness. The unknown, impecunious lawyer who spends a lifetime assiduously and effectively serving the poor can attain greatness and many already have.

And I will close with a story about Joe Carrieri, a Fordham Law School graduate. Joe was the bat boy for the New York Yankees and wrote a book entitled *Search for Heroes*. He found one in Joe DiMaggio.

Towards the end of DiMaggio's career, Carrieri asked DiMaggio to tell him the secret of success. DiMaggio didn't respond immediately but promised to do so. More than a year later, in the fall of 1951 and after DiMaggio had decided to retire, he sent for Carrieri and a highly nervous Carrieri went to Yankee Stadium to meet with the legendary Joe DiMaggio. DiMaggio told Carrieri that he was delivering on his earlier promise and said the following:

"Remember to stay interested in the game, in the game of baseball and the game of life. Enjoy the moment. Not every one can be the best, but you can give it your best. Whether it is baseball or anything else, be the best that you can be. I loved the game of baseball and gave it my very best. If you love what you do, you will find a way to do it well and always be a student. And as long as you live, you always have more to learn. If you can remember that, you'll have learned a great deal about the meaning of success."

Today Joe Carrieri is one of the foremost adoption lawyers in the United States.

Thank you and God Bless Fordham Law School.

TECHNOLOGY

We now live in a world of computers. Obviously, there are positive aspects to that development but there are negative features as well.

To play with one's BlackBerry while supposedly interacting with another person or persons is grossly insulting.

To use a handheld cell phone while driving is highly dangerous.

Employees across the country who use computers in connection with their work, use them frequently and often at length, for their own purposes during working hours. That's wrong.

Children waste endless hours engaged in playing mindless, often violent and sometimes even dangerous games.

Harassment of all kinds is commonplace and pornography of the worst sort is available.

Excessive computer use will adversely affect one's ability to speak and write. I have noticed that deficiency in many law school graduates embarking on a career in the law. In my business that's a serious handicap!

At best, it's a mixed bag!

RAIN

I love the rain! It's soft, it's gentle, it's soothing and cleansing. It's wonderful to be in bed and listen to the rain on the rooftop. God is great!

LAS VEGAS

I've been to Las Vegas many times but always on business and never by choice. It's a terrible place for numerous reasons.

While it has a few impressive features, by and large it is cheap, tawdry, glitzy, artificial and decadent.

Sex, drinking and making a quick fortune the easy way, are the dominant themes. It promotes no redeeming values, whatsoever. Physically it is sprawling, ugly and located in the middle of nowhere. It takes forever to fly there and upon arrival at the airport you are confronted with long walks, trips on escalators and trams and an endless line of people waiting for cabs. The airport is a considerable distance from the city and cab meters are calibrated to soak the rider mercilessly.

The highly touted entertainment in large measure consists of individuals who are "over the hill" such as Cher and Wayne Newton.

And the aura of organized crime, which was dominant at the time of its beginnings, lingers on. Organized crime goes where the money goes, especially when it's in the form of cash.

While gambling is the main attraction, the usual accompanying human lice are ever present such as: prostitutes, drug peddlers, con artists and pickpockets.

But the aspect that I find most depressing is watching so many people who can't afford it throwing their money away with the sad and highly unlikely hope that they will "strike it rich." Many, of course, are addicted.

And, of course, those who manage the casinos do everything and anything to encourage them to squander needed family funds. And so we find women in skimpy outfits throughout the casinos serving free drinks of all sorts to those engaged in gambling. TV coverage in the rooms is limited. And I'm certain there's a lot more going on there that I don't know about.

Aside from that, Las Vegas is a great place. By the way, Atlantic City is no better.

THE ECONOMIC RECESSION OF 2008

The deep economic recession of 2008 and the accompanying collapse of the stock market have focused attention on a number of verities.

The recession was caused in part by Congressional pressures forcing financial institutions to make mortgage loans which in many cases were not secured properly and never should have been made.

It was grounded on the obviously unattainable but nonetheless highly appealing political assertion that every American should have a home and the means to purchase one.

And so, the politicians leaned heavily on financial institutions to make subprime mortgages. At first, some financial institutions resisted but in the face of pressures to participate in profits, generated by the subprime mortgage market and importuning by politicians, both Democrats and Republicans, all folded, including Fanny Mae and Freddie Mac. Subprime loans were bundled, insured, sold and resold. The economic collapse which followed was inevitable. All efforts along the way to head it off failed.

As a result of avarice and greed on the part of financial institutions and total irresponsibility on the part of politicians, interested only in getting elected, re-elected or climbing the political ladder, irreparable financial damage has been visited on millions of Americans. Older persons will not be around long enough to participate in a recovery. Nor do they have the option of working longer than they anticipated as do those still working.

Far too few politicians act on the basis of the merits and do what is in the best interests of cities, states, the nation and the people they represent without reference to their political agendas. That's why they are held in such low regard.

And when will financial institutions recognize their solemn duty and obligation to serve the best financial interests of the people that they serve as against lining their own pockets with fees, commissions, salaries and bonuses of enormous and outrageous proportions?

Again there are exceptions but it would seem that there are precious few who fully recognize, appreciate and act upon the basic reality that many people work for a lifetime to accumulate assets to take care of themselves in retirement; to aid and assist their children and to leave something to their grandchildren when they die.

Those who provide investment advice to pension funds don't seem to understand that their primary duty is to provide retirement with dignity for the people they serve — not to make money for themselves. And the same is true of investment houses which give advice to foundations, educational institutions and other entities striving to achieve worthwhile goals.

The 2008 recession was exacerbated by the fact that Wall Street institutions hired young geniuses to fashion investment vehicles that management didn't understand but nonetheless sold with a vengeance frequently in the name of "diversification" to maximize profits for themselves. It's a very sad commentary on the society in which we live.

And then we have the mindless "bailout" whereby our Government doled out taxpayer dollars to banks in the latter part of 2008. Lack of liquidity was the problem with the economy. Small businesses which make up a huge part of our economic fabric were in desperate need of loans. When the bailout money was distributed to banks there were no limitations and no requirements whatsoever that any part of those taxpayer dollars be used for loans! And so it's been used for dividends, salary increases, bonuses and buying other banks! And if you now suggest that such bailout taxpayer money be used for loans to reconstitute the economy, the banks are "outraged" by such unwarranted interference in their affairs and boldly refuse to do so! In the meantime, we still have no liquidity. It's infuriating!

FOOTBALL

I don't pretend to be an expert on football. I have little or no appreciation for the intricate line play or the many nuances unfolding before me play after play — but you don't have to be an expert to enjoy it and I do!

For years I've attended the Army-Navy game. I love the pageantry, the cadets and mid-shipmen on parade; the martial music and the "Star Spangled Banner." Just seeing those fine young men and women renews one's trust and confidence in the future of our country.

But the element that's most exciting is the fact that both teams go all out and leave their hearts and souls on the field of battle. For both teams, the Army-Navy game is by far the most important of the season. Indeed, it's been said that it's the only game of the season. Past records going into that game mean little and both teams have won in the face of overwhelming odds.

Another wonderful feature of that game is that the teams respect each other and there is no dirty play. Almost all of the penalties called are technical in nature.

I have nothing against the Super Bowl, but I'll take Army-Navy every time. It's just more fun! Being a Marine, I, of course, root for Navy.

I also root for Notre Dame. I do so, not because I went there (I attended Holy Cross College) but for two other reasons. As I've said, my Uncle Dennis F. Shanahan was the first member of our family to go to college and he went to Notre Dame. While he never played in a Varsity game, he was a "scrub" during the Knute Rockne days! He had an enormous impact upon me when I was growing up — so much so that I named my son, Dennis, after him. Years ago I took my son, Dennis, to a Notre Dame football game in South Bend, Indiana. We visited the building in which my Uncle Den lived, the chapel in which he prayed and Notre Dame won the game. The excitement generated at Notre Dame on the day of a football game is beyond belief and I urge you to try it sometime.

The other reason why I root for Notre Dame is that in its beginnings it was the school for the immigrants: Irish, Italians, Poles, Lithuanians, and on and on. Thanks to the Fathers of the Holy Ghost and Knute Rockne, Notre Dame became highly competitive academically and in sports in very short order and remains so today.

This is Uncle Den while serving in the Navy during World War II.

I also root for Penn State in football simply because of my admiration and respect for Joe Paterno. He was cut out of the same cloth as Vince Lombardi!

For many years I have been urging Presidents of Fordham University to upgrade football and to play Army at Yankee Stadium.

The sad fact is that New York City, the greatest city in the world, has no football whatever — either professional or collegiate.

The Giants and the Jets play in New Jersey and none of New York City colleges have a football team worth mentioning except Fordham.

Vince Lombardi played at Fordham and was the Assistant Football Coach from 1947–1949. He was also the Assistant Football Coach at West Point from 1949–1954.

Such a game could appropriately be labeled "The Vince Lombardi Fall Classic."

And so, I was delighted when Father McShane S.J., the President of Fordham, recently announced that Fordham is going to upgrade football and play Army as well as a number of other colleges with respectable football teams.

I believe that a Fordham-Army game at the New Yankee Stadium will draw a huge crowd and benefit both institutions enormously over the years.

I only wish my own college, Holy Cross, would follow Fordham's lead and get back into football in a meaningful way. I believe that football is an important and valuable ingredient to college life and alumni support.

BUYING A WINTER HOME

As winters in New York have worsened, I've thought about buying a house in a warm climate for winter use.

I've decided however not to do so for two reasons:

1. Such a purchase would tie me down and inhibit me from visiting a variety of locations; and

2. I've visited some of those communities and decided that I will not buy a house in a community where my age will lower the average age of those living in the community!

GIL HODGES

Gil Hodges deserves to be in the Hall of Fame. His baseball talent, both as a player and as a manager, his leadership qualities, his personality, his unflinching integrity and his conduct on and off the field took the game of baseball to a higher level.

LICENSE PLATES FOR DOCTORS

Years ago, when I was a boy, doctors were available every day and made house calls regularly. Consequently, they were accorded special license plates bearing the letters "M.D." which allowed them to park almost anywhere to attend a patient in need.

Now, most doctors take off on weekends and many take off weekdays as well. Thus the expression, "Don't get sick on a weekend." Moreover, they never make house calls. They have forfeited the right to special license plates and such plates should be discontinued. The benefit of special plates is for the patient on those rare occasions that the MD must visit you.

TAXI CAB AVAILABILITY

My law office is located on 6th Avenue between 51st and 52nd Streets. Because of that and the varied nature of my activities, I use taxi cabs regularly. There are certain times during the day when no taxis are available. That's because all cabs go off duty simultaneously at certain times of the day. That is neither desirable nor necessary and should be corrected by the Taxis and Limousine Commission.

Chapter 18: *Reflections as One Grows Older*

As I approach the end of life I find myself going back to my roots more and more – the early days, places, events and people. I cherish my old friends more and more and feel a very deep sense of loss when I lose friends like Paul Curran, Alan Schwartz, Don Mulvihill, Jack Vaughn, Mel Glass and B. J. Harrington.

I think of being reunited with them and others like my grandfather, my boyhood pal; the mother who I barely remember; the father who was so proud of me; my Aunt Nell, the Aunt who raised me when my mother died, like I was her own son; my Uncle Tom who changed my life completely by wisely and lovingly packing me off to Jesuit boarding school; my Uncle Dennis who I admired and respected enormously for his extraordinary but quiet intelligence, private piety and love of God; Frank Hogan, who instilled in me a deep-seated appreciation for the importance of public service; Eddie Schoen with whom I grew up in the law firm in which I would spend my entire professional career; Matty Silverman, my mentor in the law; my cousin, Bill Shanahan, my buddy and frequently my protector — and a host of others.

I look forward to being with them again. I came to know the souls of all of them and I know they are in heaven.

The only question is whether I will make it!

I've reflected on that subject and have come to certain conclusions which lead me to believe that I've got a shot!

I think that the most severe transgressions we can commit are twofold:

1. Willfully and deliberately flying in the face of or turning one's back on God.

2. Willfully and deliberately inflicting serious pain and suffering on another person.

I'm a true believer and I think I'm "OK" on the first.

As to the second, I might have some "issues" — to use a modern expression which I abhor. While I have inflicted severe pain on other people it has almost always been a non-thinking response to pain inflicted upon me. Moreover, I've usually tried to repair the damage and go on. To be forgiven is one of the greatest joys in life. To forgive is an even greater joy. I've tried to do that although it's been difficult in some cases.

There are, of course, many other transgressions but none that would bring about eternal damnation — I hope.

All of these thoughts are part of the cycle of life and it's important to share them with people of all ages.

I also think that the incredible joy I now derive from my grandchildren, James, Gillian and Julia, is part of the cycle of life. They represent renewal and tomorrow! It's a great life, from beginning to end.

In 2009 I purchased a bench in Central Park for my grandchildren. This is a picture of James and me sitting on that bench. I am pointing to the plaque that proclaims that the bench is for the benefit of James, Gillian and Julia.

Having said that, I have no interest in retiring and intend to work as long as I am able.

I derive enormous satisfaction from what I do as a partner in my law firm, Bryan Cave; as Chair of Group Health Insurance and Vice Chair of Emblem Health; as the founding chair and a member of the Doris Duke Charitable Foundation; as Counsel to the Board of Trustees of St. Patrick's Cathedral chaired by Archbishop Timothy Dolan; as Chair of the Irish Hunger Memorial, and continuing involvement in political matters.

I spend a great deal of time with my dear friend, Ed Koch. We have a great time together and have come to the conclusion that there are many advantages to getting older. You have a greater body of knowledge upon which to draw; you get to the heart of a matter more quickly and solve it more readily; you assess people more quickly and more accurately, you are more appreciative and perhaps best of all — you don't have to give a rat's ass!

THE END

APPENDIX A

The family of my old and dear friend, B.J. Harrington, asked me to make some comments about B.J.'s life and especially about his devotion to our law school – and I am deeply honored to do so.

B.J. was enormously proud of the history of our law school; the founding of Fordham University by Bishop John Hughes (the dreaded "Dagger John") in 1841; the transfer of the University of the Jesuits in 1846 and the opening of our law school in 1904, over one hundred years ago. He reveled in our law school's unique traditions and special culture.

He had a clear idea of what it was, and how he wanted it to remain.

Although he viewed our law school unabashedly as a Catholic-Jesuit institution, he derived great satisfaction from the fact that its doors were open to all comers from the very outset – regardless of gender, race, ethnicity, religion or disability – and all of this, long before the word "diversity" came into vogue in connection with admissions.

Fordham Law School began admitting women in 1918. In 1924, Ruth Whitehead Whaley graduated first in her class and, became the first African-American woman admitted to the state bars of New York and North Carolina!

In 1941, our law school admitted Frances G. Berko, who was a Jewish woman with cerebral palsy when no other law school would have her!

She was admitted by Fordham Law School not because she was Jewish, or a woman, or disabled, or because of all three combined. She was admitted because she was qualified; up to the job and therefore deserving of the opportunity. She was admitted simply because it was the right thing to do. Her admission was due to the influence of basic Catholic-Jesuitical moral standards.

Despite her disability she served on the Fordham Law Review and, upon graduation in 1944, devoted her life to the United Cerebral Palsy Movement, founding state organizations in New York and Kansas. In 1981, Governor Hugh Carey named her as the State Advocate for the Disabled and she is credited with being a major force in the passage of the Americans with Disabilities Act.

B.J. entered Manhattan College in 1949. Around Christmas time in his junior year – while on the way to a date with Audrey – the woman who would later become his beloved wife and the dutiful mother of his children – he was hit by a car driven by a man under the influence of alcohol. B.J. was dragged by that car for 150 feet and was severely disabled and disfigured. Thereafter, he underwent 50 operations – yes, I said 50 – over a long extended period of time; many of which had to do with rebuilding his face. I know that almost all of you were unaware of B.J.'s early problems – and that's because he never mentioned them.

With all of that, B.J. graduated from Manhattan College on time in 1953. His degree was in accounting and he sought employment in the accounting field. He pounded the pavement relentlessly for 2 years until he finally realized that his disabilities and his appearance were major obstacles to his employment. By this time, he was married with three children under 18.

B.J.'s father died when B.J. was 12 years old, and Fr. Finian Sullivan, the Pastor of Sacred Heart Parish, B.J.'s church in Yonkers, New York, became his Surrogate Father. And so, B.J. turned to him in his hour of need. Fr. Finian urged B.J. to go to law school at night and gave him a job teaching accounting and business law at Sacred Heart High School during the day. B.J. applied and was admitted to Fordham Law School's night division.

Accordingly, B.J. always treasured our night division which down through the years has afforded people who had to work during the day an opportunity to go to law school. Many of B.J.'s classmates were immigrants or the children of immigrants.

B.J. valued highly the enormous emphasis Fordham Law School always placed on ethics – also due to the strong Catholic Jesuitical influence which has always permeated our law school.

Similarly, he was greatly pleased by the strong encouragement which the law school has always provided its graduates to engage in the public service and thereby make a contribution to the common good.

He marveled at the support which our Alumni have always provided the law school and our graduates and participated heavily in that endeavor himself.

And, he was especially proud of the great academic advances our law school has attained down through the years.

Those were some of the reasons why B.J. loved our law school and that's the way he wanted it to remain. He railed against any suggestion to remake our law school in the image of other law schools.

Upon graduation from our law school, B.J. turned once again to Fr. Finian, who assisted him in getting a job at the highly distinguished Westchester law firm of Bleakly Platt where he spent his entire legal career and ultimately became the revered chairman of the firm.

I've always been fascinated by the fact that the lives of so many persons are fashioned by early background, training and experience. That was certainly true in B.J.'s case.

B.J. Harrington never forgot where he came from or how he got to what he became. He spent a lifetime repaying the persons and institutions that benefited him early on and in the doing, enjoyed a spectacular career.

And so, as indicated, he supported our law school substantially and unstintingly. No layman in my memory did more for the Church, its hospitals, its schools, its seminaries, its charities, its leaders and its clergy. He was the finest Catholic layman I've ever known.

Through his career he engaged heavily in politics and public service at local and state levels, for the purpose of benefiting society. Among other posts, he served as the legislative counsel to Lt. Governor Malcolm Wilson who ran the "day to day" business of New York State during that era.

And, throughout his life, he aided and assisted the sick and disabled. Not surprisingly, his favorite charity was the Elizabeth Seton Pediatric Center, which reaches out and cares for the most disabled children in New York City. Until his death, he served as the Chairman of its Capital Campaign.

But with all B.J. did with his life, in my judgment he will be best remembered for his undaunted courage and his uncompromising and unflinching honesty and integrity.

He was a good and decent man and among the finest graduates that our law school has ever produced.

APPENDIX B

MR. JAMES F. GILL: President Brennan, Your Eminence Cardinal O'Connor, Your Excellency Bishop Broderick, Mayor Dinkins, Minister Smith, Ambassador Hayes, Consul General O'Ceallaigh, Governor Wilson, Chancellor Peterson, other masters of the universe seated on the dais, (Laughter) both spiritual and temporal, (Laughter) Friendly Sons of Saint Patrick, friends of the Friendly Sons of Saint Patrick, friends of the friends of the Friendly Sons of Saint Patrick. (Laughter)

Father Peterson's wonderful speech about Saint Patrick and his crew brings to mind a somewhat embarrassing moment in the life of Saint

Patrick which occurred when he officiated at the Baptismal Ceremony of one of Ireland's first Kings.

As we all know, Saint Patrick had a spike at the end of his pastoral staff to help him negotiate Ireland's rough terrain.

At the very outset of the ceremony, he inadvertently stuck his staff into the King's foot. After the service had gone on for about fifteen minutes, Patrick looked down and observed that the King's foot was in a pool of blood. He immediately withdrew his staff, apologized and said, "Your Highness, why didn't you say something?" To which the King responded, "I thought it was part of the ceremony." (Laughter)

I called Dean Mulligan this morning in Florida to wish him a happy Saint Patrick's Day. During the course of our conversation I said, "Bill, is there any substance at all to the foul rumor that Irishmen have a proclivity for alcohol?" He said, "Jim, I am afraid there is, and I discovered the scientific basis for that proclivity."

He said, "When you were a young boy, did your mother insist that you take a bath every Saturday night no matter what?" I said, "Yes."

He said, "After she dried you off, did she rub you down with alcohol in order to close your pores and thereby ward off colds?" I said, "Yes."

He said, "Young Irish boys have gone through that same Saturday night ritual for generations. Unfortunately, before those pores were able to close all the way, some modicum of alcohol worked its way into the blood stream, and that is why Irishmen have a proclivity for alcohol, particularly on a Saturday night. (Laughter) (Applause)

Last fall, I traveled to Ireland for the first time. The purpose of the trip was to see Holy Cross and Fordham play football at Limerick Stadium on Saturday, November the 16th.

During the Aer Lingus flight I took to Shannon on the Thursday before the game, the main topic of conversation was why various passengers were going to Ireland.

An English Professor mused about the literary contributions of George Bernard Shaw, William Butler Yeats, James Joyce and Sean O'Casey, and how he was looking forward to a series of lectures at Trinity College and performances at the Abbey Theater.

A young priest from Boston told us that he would be spending most of the time touring the ancient ruins of the monasteries wherein the light of Christianity was kept aglow while Europe was engulfed in barbaric darkness.

An historian regaled us with the early history of early Ireland, and spoke of his desire to visit the site where the great Irish warrior Brian Boru defeated the Vikings in 1014.

Finally, the young priest from Boston said, "Mr. Gill, tell us, why are you going to Ireland?"

Rather than admit that I was going to Ireland to watch two American colleges play a game of football, I pretended to be asleep. (Laughter)

The next day was Friday. And I decided to drive to Ballyvaughan, a small village on the west coast. I had been told by an old aunt that I might find relatives on the Gill side of the family if I were to visit that village.

When I reached Ballyvaughan, I went into its only pub for lunch and to make inquiries concerning my relatives. After ordering a pint of stout, I noticed that the only other customer was an elderly man who was standing at the end of the bar talking to himself and making strange noises.

As I stared at the old man in wonderment, the bartender leaned over and whispered to me, "Pay him no mind. That's Jeremiah Gill." (Laughter) "He's as daft as a penny watch. As a matter of fact, everyone in his family is touched." (Laughter)

My dark thoughts were interrupted when the bartender asked, "By the way, what's your name?" (Laughter)

"I'm John Hennessy," I replied. (Laughter) "I'm a lawyer from New York." At that point, I observed, out of the corner of my eye, and to my horror, that Jeremiah Gill was now genuflecting in front of the bar and blessing himself with the sign of the cross, over and over again.

"Are you here to trace some relatives?" inquired the bartender. "Oh, no," said I. "I'm just passing through." (Laughter)

"As a matter or fact, all of my relatives are from the east coast." (Laughter)

Just then the young priest from Boston, who I had met on the plane the day before, entered the pub and said in a loud voice, "Mr. Gill, how are you?" (Laughter)

I said, "I'm not Gill. I'm Hennessy." "That's strange," replied the priest, "I could have sworn that you told me that your name was Gill when we met yesterday."

At that point Jeremiah approached the priest, extended his hand, and said, "I'm Gill." Whereupon, the young priest ran out of the pub. (Laughter)

Jeremiah then approached me, looked at me intently and said in a low voice, "You look familiar, laddie. Do I know ye?" "Oh no," said I, as I started for the door, "You don't know me, and I don't know ye." And I ran out of the pub. (Laughter)

The next day I went to the football game with my friend Father O'Hare. As we were waiting for the game to commence, the young priest from Boston came up the aisle, spotted me and said, "Hello, Mr. Hennessy." (Laughter) "It's good to see you again." I said, "I'm not Hennessy. I'm Gill." (Laughter)

When the young priest was gone, Father O'Hare turned to me and said, "What was that all about?" I said, "Father, I have no idea. I never saw that man before in my life." (Laughter)

That's what we, who were trained by the Jesuits, call a "mental reservation." (Laughter)

Those of you who went to the game know that a special feature was the game announcer who apparently took it upon himself to explain the rules of American football to the Irish men and women in the audience.

For example, in the second quarter Fordham punted and a Holy Cross player, returning the punt, ran across the field laterally and was forced out of bounds.

The announcer's comment was as follows: "It was a very fine run. Unfortunately, it was from east to west. It would have been much better if it had been north to south." (Laughter)

Although very heavily favored, Holy Cross won by a mere five point margin, twenty-four to nineteen. Father Brooks, the President of Holy Cross, blessed himself so many times during the second half that I was reminded of Jeremiah Gill. (Laughter)

By the time the game was over, I had concluded that Brooks, Jeremiah and I were all related. (Laughter) That conclusion was reinforced when I saw Father Brooks talking to Jeremiah in the parking lot after the game. (Laughter)

As I drove away from the stadium I wondered whether the time would ever come when I would become John Hennessy on a permanent basis. (Laughter) (Applause)

True Irish humor has a delicious innocence to it. Many stories typify that humor. The one that I like is the story of the Irishman who came to this country many years ago and was going through immigration. Finally, the immigration officer looked sternly at the Irishman and said, "Do you advocate the overthrow of the Government of the United States by force or violence?"

The Irishman thought for a moment and said, "Violence." (Laughter) (Applause)

But 1992 is a Presidential year. And the best humor is still being produced unintentionally by American politicians. (Laughter)

Recently a candidate for the presidency was confronted with a tape recording of a telephone conversation between him and a woman claiming to be his lover of many years. The conversation was intimate in nature and included an ethnic slur aimed at Governor Cuomo. When asked about the tape the candidate said three things.

Number one: "I never had sex with that woman." Number two: "That's not my voice on the tape." Number three: "If that is my voice on the tape, I apologize to Governor Cuomo." (Laughter) (Applause)

Until then, I had no idea that the Jesuitical doctrine of mental reservation had penetrated the State of Arkansas so deeply. (Laughter) (Applause)

1992 is also an Olympic year. Although Ireland has not produced many figure skaters, a young man from Dublin competed in that category at the winter Olympics last month. No sooner was he on the ice when he fell down. And he fell down again and again throughout his performance.

All of the Judges gave him one's and two's except the Irish Judge who gave him a perfect score. (Laughter) After the event, the official in charge of the Winter Olympics sent for the Irish Judge. "That was a blatant and outrageous act of partisanship," admonished the official. "You have disgraced the Olympic games."

"There was no partisanship at all, "replied the Irish Judge. "It was very slippery out there." (Laughter)

By and large, the Irish in America have always gotten on well with the Jews and the Blacks. And that's because they have so much in common. The Jews and the Blacks have been subjected to persecution, discrimination, and misery, and so have the Irish.

In the early 1800's, Sir Walter Scott, Scotland's literary giant, referring to the abject poverty of the Irish, wrote: "Their poverty has not been exaggerated. It is on the extreme verge of human misery."

A century ago, the great William Gladstone, England's reforming Prime Minister who worked so tirelessly to provide relief for the Irish, told his Parliament, "Go to the length and the breadth of the world; ransack the literature of all countries; find if you can a single voice, a single book in which the conduct of England towards Ireland is anywhere treated except with profound and bitter condemnation." (Applause)

But I suspect the main reason that the Irish enjoy positive relationships with the Jews and Blacks is the fact that they have been so busy denigrating and vilifying the Italians (Laughter), that they just haven't had time for the Jews or the Blacks. (Applause)

But what best epitomizes the closeness of the relationship between the Irish and the Jews is the relationship between John Cardinal O'Connor and my law partner and friend, Ed Koch. (Applause)

When Ed was Mayor, they worked closely and well. They wrote a book together. They dined together regularly and continue to do so. They are the closest of friends.

Friendly Sons, I can tell you within the strict confines of this room that a development of significance has resulted from that relationship. It is a matter of religious consequence.

It is a matter which may well have profound international implications, particularly in the Middle East. It is a matter so sensitive that the Cardinal has kept it "in pectore" for the last nine months.

Of course, I am referring to the imminent conversion of Cardinal O'Connor to Judaism. (Laughter) Is he smiling? (Laughter)

While I know that this is a happy occasion, given the circumstances, I feel compelled to share with you some reflections I have had over the past several weeks about the Saint Patrick's Day Parade.

I believe that the decision by those in charge of the parade not to permit the Irish lesbian and gay organization to march in the Saint Patrick's Day Parade as a separate contingent was correct. (Applause)

There are many kinds of parades. Some are private, and some are governmental functions. Some are for the purpose of rallying support for a cause. Some are demonstrations of protest, and others are celebrations.

And so we celebrate the accomplishments of astronauts, war heroes, and athletes by parades in their honor.

The Saint Patrick's Day Parade is a private celebration. It has a significant religious component. It honors Patrick, a Saint of the Church, the Patron Saint of Ireland, and the Patron Saint of the Archdiocese of New York. It honors the Church in America.

It has a substantial Irish ingredient. It honors Ireland, the Irish who fought against English tyranny and proclaims "England Out of Ireland," (Applause) which is the only political banner and the only political cause ever authorized by parade officials since its inception in 1761. (Applause)

It commemorates the immigration of the Irish to America and reaffirms their commitment to continue their Irish culture, tradition, and heritage as American.

It is a reminder of the scalding discrimination to which Irish immigrants were subjected and of their contributions to the growth and development of this country.

And yes, it has a social element. It is a harbinger of spring. It is a day of happiness and unity. And people of all types and kinds are invited to participate in the celebration, men and women, young and old, rich and poor, Irish and non-Irish, Catholics and non-Catholics, without reference to one's beliefs or convictions, without reference to the color of one's skin, or one's sexual orientation. (Applause)

That's the way it's been for two hundred and thirty-one years; and that's the way it ought to be. No one should be excluded. But the advocacy of causes by participants in the Saint Patrick's Day Parade is an entirely different matter. (Applause)

Advocacy, and particularly advocacy of a controversial nature, has no place in such a parade. (Applause)

Because the Saint Patrick's Day Parade is a festival, every effort has been made, down through the years, to protect it against divisiveness, discord and disharmony. And those efforts should continue. (Applause)

Right-to-life organizations have not been permitted to espouse their cause as marchers in the parade, and pro-life banners have been banned despite the sacred nature of that cause to the Church.

Immigration law reform groups have not been allowed to promote changes in the immigration laws to increase Irish quotas as parade participants, despite the fact that U.S. Immigration Laws brought Irish immigration to a virtual halt from 1965 to 1986.

In past years even Joe Doherty's proponents were prohibited from urging opposition to his extradition as members of the parade, despite the traditional "England Out of Ireland" aspect of the parade, and despite the fears of many in the Irish community that Doherty would be railroaded in order to curry the favor of the English Government.

Given the fact that the Saint Patrick's Day Parade is a celebration, I believe that those decisions and others like them were correct.

And so was the decision not to permit the gays and the lesbians to march as a separate contingent. (Applause)

The presence of such a contingent would undoubtedly be perceived as advocacy and correctly so; particularly in the context of what has transpired over the past several years and continues to occur.

The Saint Patrick's Day Parade should never be allowed to become a vehicle for any advocacy group or political organization. It should not be converted into a gay rights rally or any other kind of rally. (Applause)

The Saint Patrick's Day Parade is the day in the sun for the Irish. I think that all ethnic and racial groups should have a day in the sun: Poles, Hispanics, Jews, Germans, Afro-Americans, Asians, and yes my friends, the Italians. (Laughter) Many already do.

That's what this country is all about. It is important for all of us as Americans to preserve all of those precious cultures, traditions and heritages. And they all should be celebrated in an environment which is non-partisan, apolitical, and non-adversarial. (Applause)

It would be enormously destructive and a clear violation of the First Amendment to the Constitution, which guarantees freedom of assembly, for any governmental agency to force those in charge of private parades of celebration, to include advocacy groups or political demonstrators.

Gay rights organizations have parades in New York City and in many other cities throughout the country. It is their right to conduct such parades, and that right should be honored and respected.

I guess what I am saying is, "Let's not rain on each other's parade." (Applause)

May the great Saint Patrick bless everyone in this room; particularly my own sons Patrick and Dennis.

And gentlemen, when you get to heaven and meet Saint Patrick personally, beware of his pastoral staff. (Laughter) Thank you and Erin Go Bragh. (Standing Applause)

Acknowledgement

I want to acknowledge the wise counsel and advice I received from Tim Zagat during the writing and production of this book. Thanks to him this is a much better book then it would have been if left to my own devices.